STRUGGLE

DISCOVER WHY GOD ALLOWS YOU TO STRUGGLE

MATT PILOT

Unless otherwise noted, Scripture quotations are from the New International
Version.

Cover Photo Credit: https://unsplash.com/
Text Photo Credit: https://imgbin.com/

ISBN: 978-1-5136-5995-4

Printed in the United States of America

I dedicate this book my sister, Charity. Charity was a beautiful, gifted, passionate person who loved God, loved her family and loved her special son, Joseph. Charity lived on this earth for only 36 years. Charity always trusted in Jesus to be her Lord and Savior, even as she battled through her struggles. Charity was my baby sister, whom I dearly loved. When I look at my beautiful daughter, Madison, I see so much of Charity in her. The same smile, the same passion and silliness. The same gift of music.

I want to help many Charities who also deal with their struggles. May this book encourage you to keep pressing on and keeping believing that God has a plan and a purpose for your life.

Endorsements

"Everyone struggles. But, not everyone understands the secret to mastering, managing, or rising above their struggle. In this powerful book, Matt Pilot provides insights to fix your focus, find freedom, and rise above your struggle. Want to show up and stand strong despite life's curveballs? Pick up a copy of this powerful book and learn how."

— Greg and Julie Gorman, Founders of Married For A Purpose

"Pastor Matt is one of my favorite people – he's positive, God-honoring, a hard worker and deeply loves people. He's also very honest about what it means to be human. Struggle is a real and vulnerable look at what it means to struggle... and how God intends for us to be strengthened in the process. I found this book equal parts encouraging and challenging... exactly the pastoring I need. If you are feeling stuck, sunk, scrambling or sick of striving, this book is for you!"

— Kadi Cole, Leadership Consultant, Executive Coach and
Author of Developing Female Leaders
www.kadicole.com

"Could it be that God's best for you is not to remove your struggle, but give you victory in your struggle? In his book Struggle, Matt Pilot serves as a kind of spiritual sherpa. He uses his own life journey as well as years of experience as a pastor to give us a clear roadmap for navigating life's struggles. In his book you will find truth, wisdom, help, and most of all... HOPE!"

— Lance Witt, Replenish Ministries

"Written from a personal experience which we all share, Struggle is an honest, practical guide to becoming the person God intended us to be. As a Licensed Mental Health Counselor, as well as a Certified Health Coach, I have spent countless hours over the last 25 years helping people contend for their health and well-being. I believe Pastor Matt's insights are practical and encouraging, and will be beneficial to anyone working toward physical, emotional and spiritual health. If you long to live fully and freely every day, this practical guide will help you discover your freedom in Christ."

— Kellie Agulia, Licensed Counselor and Optavia Coach

Table of Contents

Introduction

What inspired me to write this book was my dealing with so many people who are stuck with a struggle in their life. It is amazing how an individual can excel in certain areas, yet struggle in another. One would think that one success would affect another. And yet, people can be limited by one weakness or challenge in their life.

As a pastor, I hear about all kinds of struggles people face. As a person, I know intimately what it is like to struggle. I have my own. It amazes me how people can look to me for counsel and for strength, and yet forget that I am human just like them. Because of my role as a spiritual leader within my church, people seem to elevate me to a higher status. While they understand that I must have struggles, I can tell by how they approach me that they think I have life figured out. They assume I have the perfect marriage. They admire me for having great faith in God. They assume I am doing everything the right way. What people do not fully comprehend is that I am struggling with areas in my life, just as they are. In fact, it is my humanity that allows me to relate to their struggle.

It is said that teaching others allows us to learn concepts at a higher level. For, when you have to explain a concept to others, you must be able to break down complexity to simple terms. In this book, I am not trying to teach you. What I endeavor to do is to learn concepts on a higher level, and simplify them. I am actually writing this book for me and my continued growth. If you choose to read this book, you are simply coming along on the journey. Welcome aboard!

Much of my material stems from my own experience. My philosophy of writing is to share my own thoughts, my own preferences. I am not trying to prove anything to you through quoting other sources. This is not a research paper. This is not an academic work. This is a look into my life and my journey of discovery. I am telling you what has worked for me and what I am continuing to learn. While I am an avid reader and researcher, I have formed an ethos of life that I live by.

Because I am a follower of Jesus Christ, I align my ethos directly with the Word of God, the Bible. You will see a lot of teaching and example from the Bible. If you are not a believer in God, I hope you will still enjoy this book. Do not let your disagreements with religion or struggle with God distract you from being a learner. Go on the journey of discovery. Glean what you can from this. I see my writing style as primarily inspirational, not as instructional. My goal for this book is to inspire you, so that you can keep moving forward. I find that people get discouraged and too easily give up.

Lastly, I would love to hear from you. If this book touched your life in some way, let me know. The best way to do this is to find me on social media.

https://www.facebook.com/matthewpilot
https://www.instagram.com/mattpilotstuartfl/
https://twitter.com/matt_pilot

Chapter 1

Anybody have a Struggle?

Raise your hand if you have a struggle in your life.

Hands are shooting up all over the room.

How many speeches or motivational talks have you heard with the speaker asking the audience that question? Many, I am sure. Speakers who study their audience understand the importance of first connecting before communicating. One of the quickest ways they connect is by relating to people. One area that almost everyone can relate to is dealing with a struggle. Why? Because everyone has one. Everybody has had at least one area they have struggled within their life. Some areas more than others.

When you think of a struggle, what comes to mind?

You may think of some of the less "serious" struggles, like over-eating. Addiction to sugar and bread keeps you from losing weight. Maybe there is an area where you are naturally weak, like punctuality, or detail. Maybe it's that you over-commit yourself to people. These are all areas that we all have a tendency to struggle with.

Your thoughts may go to a deeper struggle in your life that you know is really hurting you.

ALCOHOLISM

Even thinking the word draws an image in your mind of a monster standing in front of you staring you down. You forgot how it started. You don't even want to think of yourself as an alcoholic, but pain has forced you to realize that you probably are one. The description fits your life, if you were honest to look and call it for what it is.

FEAR

You find that you are gripped by fear and anxiety. Fear of what? You aren't really sure. Sometimes it is there. Other times, not so much. You wonder if anybody else feels this way? It sure doesn't look like it, from how they act around you. If they only knew that you struggle with overwhelming feelings of fear. Nighttime is bad. The mornings are worse – just before you have to leave for school. For your job.

INSECURITY

Questions echo in your mind: Do I measure up? What do others think of me? Do I fit into that group of people? Will I make it? Can I handle all of this? What happens if I can't? What happens if I lose my job? What would I do if I cannot handle all that I am responsible for? Nobody would see that you have these questions rolling around inside of you. ... or...can they see them? You feel broken, not whole. Your self-esteem is fragile, and sometimes you feel like you are barely hanging on.

PHYSICAL CHALLENGE OR WEAKNESS

How about a physical challenge? A handicap of some kind? You didn't cause this. You sure didn't want it. You were born this way. Maybe it's a deformity of some kind. It makes you "different" than everybody else. And, you are so TIRED of being "different." Oh, to be able to walk into a room full of people and just... BE. To fit in. You DON'T want to be noticed. DON'T want to be stared at. DON'T want any attention.

I have struggled with a mild stuttering issue. Not particularly noticeable to most people, and maybe not clinically verifiable. But I notice. I notice that people notice, by the way they would stop...and stare...at me. I would usually stutter when I was excited or tired. Because I am an extrovert, I love to be the life of the party. I love to be the one who has something funny to say. So, when I would stutter, I got everybody's attention. But, not the attention I was going for. Awkward.

Now, this may not measure up to your struggle. You read this, and think to yourself, "that's nothing. You have no idea how bad my struggle is compared to your stuttering." I admit, the stuttering is not a major struggle for me. And, I have learned how to slow down and speak clearly. Stuttering does not happen often to me, at least anymore. But it is was a struggle for me. It can STILL BE a struggle for me when I try to talk before first thinking of what I want to say, and how I will start a sentence.

That's the thing: my struggle may not be as big as YOUR struggle. But it's big to me. It's still a struggle. I may not think much of your struggle; but to you, it's a struggle. A big one. I have had several areas in my life that proved to be a struggle for me. Some were minor, like the stuttering. Others have been major. I'm sure you have your list of struggles, just like me. Can I see your hand if you struggle? Yep. I see that hand. I see your struggle.

Struggles suck. I'm sorry. I apologize for my coarse language. I thought for a minute before writing that out. But, in looking at it, I realized that it was the best way to describe how a struggle feels. It sucks. As one of my friends would say, "it Hoovers." For those of you who are scratching your head not getting that, a Hoover is a vacuum cleaner. ....still don't get it? Ah, forget it!

Struggles are no fun. They ruin fun. Life is meant to be enjoyed, to be fully-lived, and fully realized. An ideal day should start with you jumping up out of your bed singing "O what a beautiful moooorrrrrrn-niiiiing!" You should be excited and ready to tackle the day. But a struggle sucks the life out of your day. (...that's what a Hoover vacuum cleaner does. It sucks. There you go.)

The word, struggle is a descriptive word. As I say it, I can literally visualize a picture. Like any good author, I looked up the word in the dictionary to study the official definition. Meriam Webster's Dictionary listed this definition:

struggle

1: to make strenuous or violent efforts in the face of difficulties or opposition
Example: *struggling* with the problem

2: to proceed with difficulty or with great effort
Example: *struggling* to make a living

I'm glad I looked this up. These are great definitions of what I see a struggle as being. Notice the words used to describe the title of my book, **Struggle**:

strenuous • violent • effort • difficulty
• opposition

What tough words! Wow. There is no fluff and puff here. A struggle takes energy. A struggle zaps energy. A struggle is rough and tumble. It can mess you up.

Difficulty

This is a word that really zeroes in on what I want to dive in to in this book. What makes a struggle a struggle is that it is a difficulty. Nothing about it is easy.

Ever deal with difficult people? Whenever I come face to face with a person who I realize is being difficult, I think to myself, "why can't this be easy? Why are they making this so difficult when it doesn't have to be?"

How about a difficult situation? Struggling to picture one? Let me help jog your memory:

- Get your spouse, parents, and in-laws to all agree when and where Thanksgiving dinner will be this year

- Your wife asks you if her outfit makes her look fat

- Your husband wants you to be mother, businesswoman, friend, house cleaner, wife, and lover

- Your friends at school all hate the President that you voted for

- Every time you go to print a report from your laptop, the printer shows *"not connected"*

A struggle proves difficult when you discover it challenges you. It could be an area of weakness, or something you are not good at. Other areas in your life are going just fine, because you have a handle on them. But the area of struggle always proves difficult, because you can't seem to figure it out. Your difficulty is defeating you. Over and over.

Something I struggled with a few times a year were sinus infections. When my body would get run down, my sinuses were a susceptible place where sickness would invade and grow. If you have ever had a sinus infection, you know it can be painful. The sinus pressure is acute, and the blocked sinus passages restrict your breathing through your nose, causing you to breathe through your mouth.

When I would go to my doctor for help, he would always try to convince me to let the sinus infection heal naturally, recommending therapy and rest. Because I was in so much pain, I would ask for antibiotics. They always worked. And yet the antibiotics were breaking down my immune system and weakening my body. My doctor warned me that every time I took strong antibiotics, my body would eventually build up a resistance to them so that they would not work in killing bacteria in my sinus cavity. It was a vicious cycle that I went through every year, and it took me out of work and activity for two weeks at a time.

Whenever we have a weakness, we want a solution, and quickly. We feel the pain and want to relieve it. Medicine hands us a magic pill that promises to take away the pain and make the weakness go away. But, in reality, the weakness does not go away. Actually, the weakness grows stronger as our body becomes weaker, thereby making it more difficult to treat. The stronger the weakness, the stronger the medication.

Opposition

This word speaks of the place we find ourselves when we are trying to do something good, but then find that life pushes us back. We are trying to reach higher, only to get knocked down.

Sometimes people are the opposition. Other times, it is a system we are working in that creates opposition. Many times, WE are our own worst enemy.

There is no better example of this than the struggle to lose weight. Fewer goals are harder to achieve than losing pounds. Can I hear a Pentecostal Church Amen?

I don't know many people who have NOT been on a diet to lose weight. Yes, there are a few lucky people who actually have to drink protein shakes to gain mass. If that's you, I'm sure you could share your struggle with me, and I respect that. But honestly, I cannot relate to you. I am in the 95% of society who gains weight simply by walking near a box of fresh Krispy Kreme Donuts in the grocery store. *#struggle!*

Isn't it funny how when we are maintaining our weight and eating normal, we are doing alright. But as soon as we commit to a diet, the opposition hits us like a Mac truck on the highway! We hit a wall. For some, it is on day one. For others, it's for one week. That's me. Can't get past a week.

The opposition comes in all forms and fashions. It comes from our friends and family who are eating pizza on Friday night while you are eating a dry chicken breast with cooked zucchini. It comes when you walk through the break room at work and see the pastries sprawled out to tempt your taste buds.

The biggest opposition is YOU. Your body is literally aching for carbs, cringing for sugar. Nighttime is torture. You are sitting on the couch watching tv after a long day, and you want to cry because you can't enjoy your snacking.

Is this painting a picture for you? Am I getting real? Come on somebody!

Our struggle kicks our butt. It has us whooped. At least, that is how we see it, from our vantage point.

We view our struggle like a wall that looks too high to climb over. Or, we view it like the giant, Goliath ready to fight us and oppose what we are trying to accomplish.

How do you view your struggle? Is it kicking your butt? How you see your struggle determines how you approach it.

Your struggle may be real. It may be big. But I am asking you to pause and ask the question: how do you see your struggle? How much do you fear it? How much power does it have over you?

> # How you see your struggle determines how you approach it.

If you are not careful, you can give your struggle power by how you see it in your life. Just by the very perception you have of your struggle, you may be empowering it to keep you down.

This is an IMPORTANT thought I just shared with you. Sometimes, when I am reading a book to expand my understanding, I will reread a statement a few times, so I can fully ingest it into my mind, and even let it sink deep into my spirit. You may need to reread pieces of this book back a few times.

Your view of your struggle may be the reason you are living under the weight of it.

Sexual Purity

I have had so many men share with me their struggle with purity. Sexual sin is a struggle for all men at some point in their life. Many women also share their struggles in this area of intimacy. However, my conversations have been primarily with men. The wise King Solomon wrote a lot about our struggle with sexual purity, warning his son of the trap of sexual temptation. Why did he write so much about this in the collections of Proverbs?

The first reason is likely he saw the destruction of his own father and the devastation it caused in his family. Solomon was actually born out of sexual sin, with his father, King David having a sordid affair with another man's wife, Bathseba. Solomon's father struggled with lust, and it had consequences reaching beyond just his own family, affecting the entire Kingdom of Israel.

The second reason could have been that Solomon himself struggled with lust. The Bible describes King Solomon as having all of the power and wealth a man could hope for. The problem with being a King is that there are few people who can help him stay guarded in his interior life. Solomon had access to all pleasures the world could offer, including fulfilling every sexual desire he could want. On the other side of sexual sin comes consequences.
Painful consequences. Broken relationships. Humiliation. Lost innocence. Hurting others.

Both men and women find that they grapple with sexual sin in varying ways. This intimate part of their life becomes a major area of struggle, and begins to overshadow them. The insidious part of sexual sin is that it deteriorates a person's confidence. It wounds their very identity, beating them down with pain and then shame. The pain keeps them hidden while the shame keeps them quiet.

One Man's Struggle

One man who came to me in the church where I am a Pastor was caught by his wife in sexual sin. I will call him Tom, to protect his identity. This was not the first time for Tom. He was in his sixties and was an established person in our community. Tom was a father and a grandfather. Coming from a conservative church background, Tom was at an all-time low point of shame and depression. His Christian upbringing had instilled in him the importance of living a moral life. To struggle with sexual sin, in his understanding, meant that he must not truly love God, nor was he a true follower. This may not have been taught outright from church leadership, but this was the unstated belief system within the church community that Tom grew up in.

I remember processing with Tom in my office, how he was dealing with his struggle. He used language like:

"I am just so weak. I can't help myself."

"I am a bad person. My wife doesn't deserve the pain I have caused her."

"God is upset with me. I know Christians aren't supposed to live in sin as I have been."

"It doesn't matter how hard I try, the temptation is too great."

Listening to Tom pour out his heart, writhing in pain and disgust of his struggle, I began to consider this topic of our struggles. I hated hearing Tom feel so defeated. While I agreed with Tom that his sin was destroying his life and family, I knew that just caring for him in his struggle would not help him find freedom.

> # What is weak will break.

Although I offered him my support and prayer, I knew that Tom needed tools to help him grow so that he could overcome in this area of his life. He needed more than just healing. He needed strengthening. If Tom simply healed but did not build strength in this area of his life, he would fall again. It would only be a matter of time. As soon as stress comes and as soon as wounds surface, the damaging habits and impulses would take over, sooner or later. What is weak will break.

Injury Causes Insight

I learned a valuable lesson from an injury I incurred while playing basketball. Growing up, I played a lot of basketball. I loved it. My younger brother and I played in the front driveway of our house for hours at a time.

As I left for college, I continued my habit of playing pick-up games in the school gymnasium on campus. The games moved faster, playing full-court with some varsity players. As my body was bigger, and as I jumped higher, I started landing wrong and would roll my ankles. The first few times, I would just walk it off and keep going. Being young and uneducated, I did not understand the importance of letting my body properly heal. Not being a serious athlete, I was not interested in body conditioning and strengthening. While others would get to the game early to stretch, I would just show up ready to play at tip-off.

I remember one game when I came down hard and landed wrong on another player's foot. My ankle rolled bad. It was painful. The guys carried me off the court. One of my friends called my then-girlfriend, Kellie Burns to come get me.

By the time Kellie arrived at the gym, my ankle had swelled to the size of a large cantaloupe. She made the decision to take me to the emergency room. The nurse gave me ice packs, wrapped the ankle and gave me crutches. They gave me directions on how to care for my ankle, which I did not pay attention to (maybe because my girlfriend was so beautiful, I could not see anything else ☺).

My ankle eventually healed and life moved along. But, after that episode, I would continue to roll my ankles. It happened in basketball games. As I got older (and as I gained weight from an unhealthy diet), I rolled ankles just walking.

The next time I remember injuring my ankle was when I was in my thirties. As a Pastor, I would make visits to the local hospital to pray for people within our church family. Walking outside the hospital entrance, I tripped over a curb and rolled my ankle so bad, that I fell over in pain. Two strangers nearby ran over to help me. One ran into the hospital and grabbed a wheelchair. I could not believe that I found myself here as a young man, having to be pushed in a wheelchair like an elderly person! The sprain was so bad, that my now-wife, Kellie was taking me (again) to a doctor to help me heal. However, this time, she found a foot specialist and scheduled an appointment.

This foot specialist was exactly what I needed. He did not just wrap my foot and tell me to keep ice on it. He did not just prescribe strong pain medication and send me home. This specialist insisted that I understand why I was continuing to struggle with rolling my ankles. He showed me pictures of the foot muscles and the bone structure. He showed me how the tendons support the movement of the foot and the weight of my body.

He would not just help repair the damaged foot, he would help strengthen the healed foot.

Don't Just Heal, Strengthen

At this time in my life, I had also become friends with a chiropractor. When he saw the boot on my foot, he asked me about what happened. I told him about my accident. My friend reinforced what the foot specialist had taught me about therapy. "I would be glad to do physical therapy on your foot once it is fully healed. Let's get those ankles strong."

Let's Get Those Ankles Strong

This was a new concept for me. I had never thought to work on strengthening my ankles. Nor did I realize that the best way to safeguard from rolling my ankles was to strengthen the muscles surrounding my feet.

I remember beginning the exercises with my friend on his chiropractic bench. He would push against my foot and then told me to push back. I could hardly move against his palm which he dug into my foot. Wow. I was weak! He made me work, having me push at every angle that my foot could move.

That experience with the foot specialist and my friend, the chiropractor, did more than just heal my damaged foot. I strengthened my feet. I worked on both ankles.

Since that time, I have NEVER rolled my ankles. Not once. And, I play basketball once a week with my son and friends. Full court. Fast running. High flying. (well, not Lebron James, but kind of.)

The reason I share this experience with you is that I believe it offers insight into the man who was ashamed of his struggle. Tom was defeated. Tom was at a loss as to how he should deal with his struggle. He was simply coming to me for care and support. What I decided to give him was that, and a lot more.

The Secret is in the Strengthening

What I shared with Tom is that the secret to overcoming his struggle was in strengthening areas of his life. He didn't need to strengthen shame. He didn't need to keep asking for forgiveness day after day. What he needed to do was to heal, and then strengthen. He needed to strengthen the muscles in his life that would support him in this area of sexual temptation.

I am happy to report that Tom is in a much better place in his marriage. Tom healed from the damage he caused to himself and to his family. And because he strengthened his interior life and built support systems in his exterior life, he is beginning to experience freedom. Honestly, when I met with Tom and his wife in the beginning, I did not think their marriage would make it. I am so pleased to see Tom and his wife sitting together in church worshipping Jesus, with heads held high! Only Jesus can do that! Jesus has done great work in Tom's life!

I believe you can overcome your struggle. I believe you can actually have victory over your struggle. You don't have to just live with rolling your ankles. You don't just have to live in shame and humiliation, thinking that life is always full of pain.

I want to change the way you see your struggle. I want to change how you view yourself in relation to your struggle. Do you just see it as the big, mean giant that is always going to defeat you? Do you see it as the people that are out to get you? Do you believe that it is the world that is trying to oppose you and keep you down?

That kind of thinking won't strengthen you. That mindset won't help you overcome.

This book is dedicated to all of the people with weak ankles. Weak mindsets. Weak muscles. This book is for damaged people. It's for damaged lives. If you have ever felt like your struggle has had you stuck, has had you pinned down, keep reading.

I am sharing from my own life experience. I am pointing you to people in the Bible who have had real struggles.

As you turn the page to the next chapter, I am praying for you. I am praying that God would open up your mind. I am praying that you would have the trust to open up the wound deep within you and let God use this book to heal you. And *strengthen* you.

**I can do all things through Christ who
gives me strength.**
Philippians 4:13 BSB

Chapter 2

The Struggle Remains

How many times have you prayed for God to heal you of your struggle?

I am ashamed to admit that I sometimes think to pray ONLY AFTER I am worrying about something that is a concern in my life. My prayer starts with:

"Lord, help me with this!"

"Take this away!"

"Heal me, Lord, so that I can do what You have called me to do!"

Sound familiar?

Our prayers SHOULD be prompted by our awareness of how GREAT GOD is, not how GREAT our STRUGGLE IS.

Thank God that He hears our prayers, even when
we don't start the right way, or pray the right
way. He cares for us very much, and is
attentive to our cry.
Psalm 34:15

A Real Example

I am so thankful that the Bible is full of stories of people who had struggles. I am so glad that I can find some real people who were weak and sinful, who lacked understanding and faith...

like me.

If you have not picked up a Bible in a long time, or never once, I encourage you to begin reading it. Study it. You will be surprised by how relatable it is to you.

One of the writers of the Bible was very relatable. He was real. Real screwed up!

He was a murderer. He lived in judgement of people. He lived in opposition of Jesus. Wow! That is about as anti-Christian as you can get.

This murderer-turned-author was named Saul. When Saul had an encounter with Jesus, everything changed. Jesus changed his name. And Jesus changed his game.

Saul was now Paul. Paul was no longer killing Christians, He was making Christians. With the same passion and drive that Saul had to *attack* Jesus, Paul was now *SHARING* Jesus.

Paul was driven. He was on a mission. Jesus had called Paul to share the Gospel message, the good news that Jesus is alive and has come to renew the relationship between God and man. Paul was educated and gifted, which made him effective. He was also passionate, which made him committed.

However, Paul was human. Paul was a man, just like you and me. That means, he was not without sin. He was not exempt from weakness. He was not perfect. Paul was called by Jesus. Anointed like Jesus. But He was not Jesus. He was Paul. The man.

Paul shares with us the shadow side of his life. Because Paul wanted to be real and authentic to those he preached to, he opened the veil of his inner struggle. Yes, Paul had a struggle. A man on mission had a mess he had to manage.

> ## A man on mission had a mess he had to manage.

Paul lets us in on his prayer life, showing an interesting conversation he has with God:

> ...I was given a thorn in my flesh, a messenger of Satan, to torment me. Three times I pleaded with the Lord to take it away from me. But he said to me, "My grace is sufficient for you, for my power is made perfect in weakness."
> 2 Corinthians 12:7-8 NIV

You mean to tell me that God denied Paul's request to heal him? You mean to tell me that God let Paul's struggle remain? I thought Jesus heals. I thought the Bible says "By His stripes, we are healed." What about that?

Does this mess with your theology? What do you do when Satan is allowed to torment you, and God doesn't do anything about it?

If you have read all about Paul's life in the Bible, you see God comes through for Paul later on. But I am still stuck on the fact that Paul was asking God to remove his "thorn in the flesh." I don't think Paul was being selfish here. In Paul's mind, he was on mission for Jesus. Paul was sharing

Jesus and being persecuted because of it. He risked his life in hostile environments. He was boldly declaring Jesus in a dark, pagan society. Paul even gave up his status in the religious Jewish community that he had grown up in. Paul was like the Summa Cum Laude of Yale University. He was the star pupil of his class, voted most likely to succeed. Yet Paul had given up comfort to pursue calling.

You have to put yourself in Paul's shoes to understand his prayer. I don't think Paul accepted God's answer easily. In fact, we know he didn't. He kept going back to God telling Him "you got it wrong, Lord! I need this fixed. I need you to do something." It's one thing to ask God to forgive you when you are going the wrong way and living for yourself. But when you are trying to follow God and are serving Him the best that you can, and THEN ask God to do something for you? That feels different.... Come on now. Quid Pro Quo.

Thorn in the Flesh

Paul does not tell us what his "thorn in the flesh" was. Was it a sin? Was it a weakness? Maybe it could have not been a sin, but a sickness. If it was sickness and not a sin, does that make it less offensive to God?

Why does Paul not tell us what the thorn is? Why does it matter?

Maybe Paul was embarrassed by his struggle. Maybe sharing that he had a struggle was painful enough, without describing it in detail. Wouldn't that be just like you? Just like me?

Hey there – anybody care to hang out their dirty laundry for the church to see this Sunday? Do you want to show us your internet browser history? Do you mind if I ask your spouse and your kids to tell us some of the juicy details of your struggles?

A struggle is a struggle. It doesn't matter if it is alcohol, drugs, gambling, sex, money. It can be anger, fear, worry, gossip. It can be cancer, diabetes or being overweight. It can be something that happened TO YOU. Sexual abuse, neglect. No father. Judgmental mother. Low self-esteem. Lack of self-identity.

Your struggle is *your* struggle. It may not seem like a big deal to your friends. Your family thinks you are just weak. Immature. But you are living with this struggle. And it is your business. You are dealing with the pain of it, and you get to decide how much to share. You get to decide who you want to trust with it. I respect that. Totally.

This passage in II Corinthians 12:7-8 is the *key verse* I want to focus this book on. I am SO GLAD Paul was willing to open up a wound in his own life and reveal how God responded. God did not choose to remove the wound. Rather, He worked *in* the wound.

> God did not remove the wound. He worked *in* the wound.

Friend, I wish I could tell you that God will remove your pain. But, He might not. I would love to lay hands on you and pray right now that God would bring you comfort. Sometimes He does comfort us. But, sometimes He allows the pain to remain.

What God does do is SHOW UP. God always shows up.

God is a very present help in times of trouble.
Psalms 46:1

God Conversation

When you talk to God, God will talk back. That's what prayer is. Prayer is a conversation with God. Don't let prayer just be a one-way monologue from you to God. Don't do all of the talking and none of the listening. Or, sometimes we do the opposite. We do all of the listening and do none of the talking. We may sit in church and hear God's Word being taught, but we never engage in conversation with God.

Paul had invited God into His life. Paul had cultivated a relationship with God, which means He had ongoing conversations with Him. That is called a prayer life. It's more than just a prayer before dinner. It means spending time talking with and listening to God. Your Heavenly Father.

I digress. But I am glad I did. God wants to share some beautiful things with you. He wants to do something awesome in your life! He has so much more for you. He stands at the door of your heart and knocks. When you invite Him in, He will enter. And He will bring healing and life and power that you have never experienced before!

Look! I stand at the door and knock. If you hear my voice and open the door, I will come in, and we will share a meal together as friends.
Revelation 3:20 NLT

My Grace is Sufficient For You

The reason God did not remove Paul's thorn was that God wanted to do something great in Paul's life. God could have removed that painful, irritating thorn. Then, Paul would have been free to fulfill His calling by Jesus. Or, so Paul thought. However, God was not interested in just using Paul's life. God was interested in working IN Paul's life.

There is nothing more inspirational than a story of a person who has overcome a struggle. What makes a hero? It is their struggle. Seeing someone overcome moves us to want to overcome in our own lives. It is not inspiring to just be great. The overcoming is what makes us great.

> **The overcoming is what makes us great.**

God was going to work in Paul's weakness. God was going to show His great power in the middle of Paul's struggle. We must always remember that we can do nothing great without the power of Jesus Christ living in us. He who called us will empower us. When we realize our need for God, we will remain dependent on God.

God has a calling on your life. Yes. You. God has created you with a purpose and a destiny. (Proverbs 3:5) You are created to perform awesome works, for the single purpose or revealing God's Son, Jesus Christ to the world. (Ephesians 2:10) Yet, you know you have a struggle that is keeping you from fulfilling that calling. The struggle has weakened you and left you discouraged. How can you possibly stand in your calling when you are struggling?

The word, grace means *undeserved favor*. God said to Paul "My grace is sufficient for you." God wanted me to tell you, right now in this book:

> I give you grace for your struggle. I give you My favor. I know you don't think that you deserve it...after what you have done...your sin and your struggle...your weakness or your hurt. But I choose to give it. **Grace** on you. **Grace** on your life. **Grace**

> ## Grace catches us. God will never let you sink.

over your sin. **Grace** over your struggle. I free you in the Name of Jesus. I free you of your struggle. I am now breaking the chains that your struggle has over you. In the Name of Jesus. You will indeed begin to stand back up in your calling.

You will begin fulfilling the purpose I have for you. I have not forgotten you. I have not left you. I am with you. I am the God that is a very present help in your trouble. In your struggle. I am here. I will not leave you. I am just getting started in your life. You thought it was over. It is the beginning!

Receive that word over your life today, in Jesus Name. I don't care what you have done. I don't care how low you are. I don't care where you have been. God used a man named Saul who was a murderer and an enemy of Jesus and turned His life upside down. Actually, God turned Him RIGHT SIDE UP!

Grace Before Greatness

God's grace was given to Paul so that Paul could discover that he had the potential to grow stronger. Paul had muscles he did not know he had. There were skills that he had not yet learned, wisdom that he had not yet discovered. Paul had learned the Scriptures as a young man from a religious standpoint. But God was going to show Paul some practical insight into the Scriptures that would enable Paul to build his life stronger. For Paul to sustain the pace of his ministry and to withstand the thorn that Satan was attacking him with, Paul was going to have to build some muscles.

God's grace is given to us when we fail. His grace is given to us freely and liberally, to apply to the weak areas of our lives. But God's grace is not intended for us to keep living in weakness and in struggle. (Romans 6:1-4) God has a bigger design intended for you and for me.

God's grace is available to you whenever you need it. And God's greatness is ready for the taking. He has designed you for victory. He has made you to be a Champion. A Warrior. Jesus lived a victorious life. He conquered sin. Defeated Satan. Rose from the grave. If Jesus is the hero that we are to model our lives after, we are also called to live in victory. (Romans 8:31-39)

Think of grace working like a parent who holds their child in the swimming pool. When our kids are small, we hold them close to us as we wade in the water. Because our kids are still learning to swim, they feel the need to hold on to us. They hate the feeling when they are sinking in the water, with no parent close to catch them. So, as good parents, we stay close and catch them when they feel like they are sinking.

Grace catches us. God will never let you sink. When you stay close to Him and hold on to His hand, He will never let you drown. He will hold you up. However, just like we want our kids to learn to swim, God wants us to learn to build the muscles and learn the skills to swim in the water.

I remember teaching my two kids to swim. We would all go as a family to our local pool in the summer. As I felt my kids were ready for a challenge, I would allow them to swim for a few seconds without me holding on to them. They would struggle to swim and start to sink, and I would immediately catch them and pull them up. They would be a little shaken, and my wife would be yelling, "Daddy! Be careful with my babies!" My wife is a nurturer, where I am the developer. She was always making sure I was not pushing our kids too hard.

Kellie and I balance each other out. I have to remind her that in order for our kids to grow, they have to be given space to struggle. If we always comfort them and solve their problems, they will never develop muscles. I would argue with Kellie in the pool "how am I supposed to teach them to swim if they don't know what it feels like to swim on their own?"

Kellie could not argue with me, but she could not stand to watch. A good mother struggles to see her children struggle. But I wanted our kids to experience what other kids were experiencing: Fun swimming on their own. I wanted them to be able to swim freely. I wanted them jumping in the pool on their own, yelling "Dad, look! Cannonball!"

In order for them to get there, I had to wean them off of my support and let them learn a skill. To learn how to swim, they would first have to learn by struggling in the pool. So, every summer, as they got older and more confident, I would give them more space away from me to branch out and swim farther. I would stand in the pool close to the edge and have them jump into me. When they finally swam to me and I pulled them up out of the water, they were so proud. They swam without me holding on to them. I cheered for them. Kellie cheered for them, sitting over in the distance, with one eye open covering her view. My children could swim like fish!

My strength had held my kids in the pool when they did not yet have their own strength. But my willingness to let them struggle in the pool allowed them to work their unused muscles and learn the skill of swimming. As a loving father, I would never let my kids sink too far, too long. I take no joy in seeing my children suffer. But I know that struggling forces strengthening. To survive, we must strengthen the skills necessary to survive. This is not brutal. This is life.

Struggling forces strengthening.

Many people go through life never embracing their struggle. They just sit on the sidelines, holding on to anything or anybody that will hold them and pick them up. They never grow. They never succeed.

Rise Up

When Jesus would heal people, He would do it by giving a command.

In the book of Luke, Chapter 5, we see Jesus in a crowd of people encountering a man that was on the ground, stranded there because his legs would not work. Jesus asked him "do you want to be well?"

The man explained to Jesus how other people were blocking him from getting to a pool nearby that was said to have healing properties. He was waiting on someone to pick him up and carry him to the pool. He thought "if I could just get in the water, then I would be healed." The lame man's thinking was wrong. His healing would never come by carrying. It would only come by strengthening.

Jesus ignored the man's *lame* response and gave him a command. "Rise up, pick up your mat and walk." The Bible then says that the man stood up, picked up his mat and walked.

This is interesting. Jesus did not do what the man was implying. When Jesus asked "do you want to be well?" The man did not say "Yes! Tell me what to do and I will do it!" Rather, the man began explaining his problem to Jesus.

Stop there. Are you explaining your problem to Jesus? Are you reminding Jesus that you have a struggle? Do you think He does not understand what you are dealing with?

Jesus did not ask the man "what is your problem, and how can I help?" Jesus cut right to the main issue: "do you want to be well?"

God is confronting you with this question for your struggle: do you want to be well?

God doesn't need an explanation of your struggle. Stop glorifying your struggle. Stop giving focus and energy to your problem. You are just making it bigger in your life. God is bigger than our struggle. God is offering to make you well.

Jesus' response to the man was a directive. Jesus commanded him to rise up. The man was hoping Jesus might carry the man over to the pool so that the man could be first in line for a miracle. "Maybe the pool will take away my pain. Maybe I will just miraculously feel better."

Yet, Jesus' command took some major action on the part of the man. Jesus was calling the man to some "big first steps." The man had to stand up. He had not stood up for many years. His legs likely had no muscle mass. He had no balance. He did not have any cane or support system he could lean on. He had to stand up on his own two feet. Then, he had to bend down, pick up his mat and walk away. Even more difficult. The Bible does not say that Jesus carried Him away. The man *walked* away. On his own.

I don't know how this miracle unfolded, more than what the story shares in scripture. What the Bible does say happened was:

1. Jesus said "rise up"
2. The man stood up, took his mat and walked away
3. The man was healed and could now walk

I don't know if Jesus caused the man's legs to grow immediately. Or, maybe Jesus gave the man faith to walk until his legs would eventually grow stronger. What I do notice is that Jesus directed an action. And, when the man took action, he was able to walk away completely on his own.

Jesus is speaking deliverance from your struggle. Freedom from your sin. He says *Your sins are forgiven you. Go and sin no more.* Jesus forgives. Now start living and stop sinning. For your struggle, Jesus commands you to *Rise Up.* Your first step is to rise up. As you take your first step over your struggle, you will begin

> ## Steps Build Strength.

growing stronger. Steps build strength. Jesus will speak healing. But it takes you to walk in that healing.

Now, I don't want to get into a theological debate with you about how Jesus heals. I know Jesus will also heal instantaneously. What I am pointing out, however, is a very important part of living the Christian life in an authentic way. There are many people who love Jesus and are trying their best to follow Him, but remain stuck in their struggle. They are beaten down by thinking that they are bad people because they are struggling. I want to give practical teaching that I see revealed in God's Word that helps people overcome sin, addiction, sickness and hurts. We see in the Apostle Paul's life a great example of being weak, flawed, forgiven, and yet focused on Jesus. He lived an overcoming life, and he did it with a thorn in his side.

> *I have fought the good fight.*
> *I have finished the race.*
> *I have kept the faith.*
> 2 Timothy 4:7 NIV

Like Paul, we can live a life of freedom. We can overcome our struggles. Yes, in some cases, Jesus chooses to remove pain and struggles in our life. But many times, He allows struggles to remain in us to develop us. To strengthen us. To teach us.

> Therefore I will boast all the more gladly about my weaknesses, so that Christ's power may rest on me. That is why, for Christ's sake, I delight in weaknesses, in insults, in hardships, in persecutions, in difficulties. For when I am weak, then I am strong.
> 2 Corinthians 12:9-10 NIV

Could it be that the first step to freedom over your struggle....is to struggle? Could it be that as Jesus is speaking healing into your life, that He is commanding you to "Rise up, take up your bed and walk?" That first step will feel like a struggle. It won't feel like healing, at least what you think healing feels like. It will be hard. Painful. Difficult. Opposition. Remember those words?

Conclusion

In the first chapter, I wanted to give you fresh hope that you can indeed experience victory over your struggle. I wanted to change your view of your struggle, not as it standing over you; but, with you standing over it.

In this second chapter, I wanted to show you how God will allow your struggle to remain in your life for the purpose of strengthening you so that you can overcome it. I wanted to show you what healing looked like in the Bible; how Jesus commanded a lame man to rise up and walk. Jesus spoke healing. The lame man had to walk in healing. And the first step in healing will feel like a struggle.

This next chapter is going to show you the power of focus. It is difficult to focus when we are feeling defeated. However, focus is vital when we begin taking our first steps in overcoming our struggle.

Chapter 3

Fix Your Focus

> Therefore, since we are surrounded by such
> a great cloud of witnesses, let us throw off
> everything that hinders and the sin that so easily
> entangles. And let us run with perseverance the
> race marked out for us, **fixing our eyes on
> Jesus**, the pioneer and perfecter of faith. For the
> joy set before him he endured the cross, scorning
> its shame, and sat down at the right hand of the
> throne of God. Consider him who endured such
> opposition from sinners, so that you will not
> grow weary and lose heart.
> Hebrews 12:1-3 NIV

What you see is what you get.

How you look at something determines what it means to you. Something can become *something* in your life. A hurt can become bitterness growing inside of you. A criticism can become a wound to your self-esteem. A struggle can become a limit to your potential.

Hurts and criticisms are all bad. I will give you that. Struggles do not seem supportive to us, at least in a positive, life-giving way. Hurts hurt. Criticisms tear us down. Struggles hold us down.

It is how we see our struggle that makes the difference in how we approach it. We give our struggles power; either power to hurt us, or to build us. That is what I want to show you in this book. I want to show you how you can use the struggle or hurt in your life to *build* your life.

In the Book of Hebrews Chapter 12, the writer, Paul points us to his example, Jesus. Paul had set himself up to the earlier Christians as an example to follow. Paul said "follow me as I follow Christ." 1 Corinthians 11:1. Paul was pointing to Jesus' life and struggle. Jesus was unique from all humankind, in that, though he was fully man, He was able to live a perfect life, without sin. Yet, even Jesus had a struggle. His struggle was the burden He faced by taking on the sins of the world.

If you are reading this and your struggle is something that happened TO you, consider Jesus. I am sure you could share with me your own struggle with sin. But you know, or you may have been told that your struggle stems from things that happened to you. Let me tell you that Jesus understands. Jesus did not cause the sin He had to carry to the cross. Jesus did not deserve His struggle. Yet, He had to face His struggle. And, Jesus showed both you and me that He endured to the end, living victoriously.

The Apostle Paul gives us the formula to overcome our struggle. He instructs us to *fix our eyes on Jesus*. Look up! Focus on our Savior, Jesus Christ! He is a good example. He is our perfect example. We can look at His life and see that it is possible to live in victory over our struggle. We see that Jesus' struggle did not make Him bad. He was actually

> Your struggle does not define you. It is left there to build you!

perfect. It is possible for a person to experience a struggle, and yet still love God and live for Jesus. It is possible for a Christian to follow Jesus as best as they know-how, and still struggle. There is nothing wrong with you. There is nothing sick about you. You belong to God, and you are a child of God. You are bought with the precious blood of Jesus Christ, the moment you put your faith in Him! Your struggle does not define you. It is left there to build you!

When you and I have surrendered our lives to the Lordship of Jesus Christ, we identify with Him. We belong to Him. The Bible says we are a new creation. The old is gone, and the new has come! 2 Corinthians 5:17. This is a fundamental truth that we must accept and live by. We are no longer defined by our sin or our struggle. *We are defined by Jesus.* We are headed in the same direction as Jesus. We are headed toward victory, toward freedom. He now becomes our compass, our focal point. If we follow him, step by step, struggle to strength, we will reach the joy that is set before us! We will experience the life that Jesus promises to give us!

You're Not Sick

A few years ago, I started going to a chiropractor more regularly. He and I became friends. He is a believer in Jesus. He not only believes in holistic, natural healing for the body, He believes that healing comes from Jesus.

One day, I was struggling with sickness when I visited him. It was a time when I was struggling with a sinus infection. When I told him about the antibiotics I was taking, he gently scolded me. He took me into his office before adjusting me. He showed me that chiropractic therapy was not like medicine that numbs the body from pain, or kills bacteria in the body like antibiotics. Chiropractic therapy rather aligns the spine and body to maximum efficiency so that the systems in the body can work the way God created it to work.

When I mentioned again my sickness, he corrected me by saying "you're not sick. You're healthy. Don't say that you're sick." Bill explained "your body is responding the way it should naturally to get healthy again. Your sinuses are inflamed and are draining to get the bacteria out. Your temperature is higher so that your body can kill the bacteria."

I argued with him "Well, I sure feel sick." He answered "if your body was sick, it would not be doing what it is doing to fight off the bacteria. What you are feeling is your body working to get healthier."

This was transformational for me. Rather than thinking that I was sick with a sinus infection, I was changing my perspective that my body was doing something very healthy. It was properly attacking bacteria.

Bill began urging me to grow healthier in my lifestyle. He told me that the healthier my body was, the stronger my immune system would become, thus fighting the infection before it grows in my sinuses. Cutting out sugar and bread was key. Not only do eating sugar and bread cause weight gain, they also cause inflammation in the body, and destroy your immune system.

My wife and I both got serious about our health, as we both began visiting our chiropractor regularly. He would reinforce healthy habits and hold us accountable. Not only were we getting regular adjustments to our spine, we were eating healthier and were exercising. Of course, when one area of your life gets healthy, it affects other parts. Our sleep improved. Our rest improved. Our emotions improved. Our stress levels diminished.

I am thrilled to tell you that I have not had a sinus infection in five years! When my body does get run down, I experience minor nasal congestion and fatigue for just two days at the most. I rebound stronger as I take time to rest.

Now, I am not going to start writing out a weight loss plan with recipes and workouts. I am hardly qualified to be a health coach. While I have been able to achieve some life goals for weight and health, it is an area that I still have to manage. I will address the need to manage our struggles in a later chapter. The take-away for me sharing this insight is this: *Focus on your health, not your struggle.*

> # Focus on your health, not your struggle.

Don't see yourself as sick. See yourself as healthy. When you observe your struggle from a larger perspective, you begin to understand and embrace that you really are healthy. You simply need to fight off your struggle. To do this, you have to focus on getting healthier. Focus on getting stronger. Here is why:

Focusing on your sickness and struggle does not build you up. All it does is pull you down. Giving attention and talk to how bad your struggle is only discouraging you. It does nothing positive for you. However, focusing on the fact that you are healthy and whole carries a positive mindset that is empowering. Remember that you are a new creation in Christ. You can do all things through Christ who gives you strength. Even difficult things. When you fix your eyes on

Him and His example, it pulls up your focus. Jesus pulls you up to Him. Jesus pulls you up and builds you up in His power and strength! This is what gets you stronger and healthier to overcome your struggle.

The Space of Perspective

Focus happens in the space of perspective. In this chapter, I am challenging you to change your perspective and your focus.

Your perspective is controlled by the space it is given. Think of perspective like a smartphone. When you try to read a document on your smartphone, what you can actually view is very small. Even when you zoom in on a few words of the document, you still cannot effectively read the information. This is why tablet devices were invented. Because people wanted a mobile device that they could still read news articles or watch videos with a wider perspective. The size of the screen widens the perspective of the viewer.

> When we are stuck in our struggle, our perspective becomes narrow

In relation to our struggle, when our perspective widens, we can see what is happening and how better to address it. When we step away from the pain of our struggle, we can see the beginning from the end. We can see the progress we are actually making in growing stronger. We can assess what has worked and what has not worked in our attempts to find freedom. Taking time to read this book is actually widening your perspective, so you can expand your understanding and learn about your struggle and yourself.

The problem is that when we are stuck in our struggle, our perspective becomes narrow. We are too close to see objectively the mess we are in. All we see is that we are stuck. All we feel is shame. All we experience is depression and hopelessness. Our perspective tells us that we will always be a servant to our struggle.

Tight Spaces

Your perception is vital to your being able to focus on getting stronger. You need to keep a wide perspective. Be careful not to get yourself into a tight space; that is, isolating yourself from others. Staying distant from people keeps you in a tight space. When you are struggling, you will want to hide. It is the shame and depression that pulls you down and makes you feel all alone. Your perception of truth is distorted when the only perspective you can see is your own. Your point of view is just that. Just yours. That is a narrow vision. That will keep you defeated. You need others to give you a wider perspective.

To widen your perspective, you need to *push yourself* to interact with some positive people. When you are feeling down and ashamed, this is the last thing you *feel* like doing. But it is the BEST thing for you. Invite people into your life. Initiate conversation with people you see as positive people. Don't look for perfect people. There are none. Rather, look for people with great attitudes. There are many. Insert yourself in their life. Get where they are at. Be a part of what they are doing.

Being with people does not mean that you need to start sharing immediately about your struggle. On the contrary, I advise against that. That will chase positive people off. Rather, get moving with the right crowd, and your perspective will start to change. This may not make sense at first. You so badly want to spill your guts and tell someone about your troubles. I understand that. And that opportunity will come. I think it is necessary to share your struggle...but at the right time.

Remember that a wide perspective allows you to focus on health, not struggle. I am arguing that what you need, especially in the beginning is a change of focus from your struggle.

As a Pastor, I had the privilege of launching a couple of churches in Florida. I love the church and believe in the strategy of what the church provides for people. Launching a church often requires starting in a rented facility within the community. Rarely does a church start with a beautiful, new building.

We started Christ Fellowship in the Stuart community in Martin County. We were able to rent the local high school to meet on Sundays. We would bring in our mobile equipment from a storage facility every weekend and set up church. It was exciting to be worshipping Jesus and teaching God's Word in a local high school. However, it took a lot of work. We had 50 road cases that we unloaded and transported in so that our volunteers could help us set up for the Sunday service. As you can imagine, volunteers can be hard to come by. Consequently, I was always looking to recruit people to come help me set up and tear down.

Many Sundays, I would meet people who we're dealing with a struggle in their life. Divorce. Alcoholism. Drugs. Job loss. Pain. Loneliness. You name it, I heard it.

Our church was established in Stuart for this very reason: to help people who are far from God find God. We were there to lead them to Jesus so that they could find healing. When people find their identity in Jesus, they soon discover God's purpose for their life.

As I would listen to their needs, one by one, I would pray with them and care for them. What I would always do is invite them to join me in helping with the setup and tear down. At first, they would give me a funny look, as if to say "how is me setting up church going to help with my struggle? I just lost my job. I am separated from my wife." I would invite them just the same and told them to trust me. I told them that I could spend more time with them this way, which they were asking for anyway. I told them that I have some great people on our team that I want to connect them to.

Many whom I invited would not come...but some would. And here is what happened with those that actually accepted my invitation: their perspective widened. Their circle of friends changed. Their spirit was renewed. While their circumstances did not change initially, their perspective changed dramatically.

> ## Serving others lifts your spirit and brightens your attitude.

There is something powerful about serving someone else's needs that changes your focus. When you serve with other great people around you, it lifts your spirit and brightens your attitude. While you may be losing in your struggle at home, you are winning in serving in your church. You belong to a winning team. Serving gives you a fresh perspective, that your life has bigger meaning.

These precious people who committed themselves to sweat and serve with me began seeing breakthroughs in their struggles. They would come to me on Saturday mornings with a huge smile to tell me how God is working in their life. They were 6 months sober. They had found a job. Their spouse no longer wants a divorce. One young man and young woman who were single met each other through serving and eventually got married!

The same can happen for you. You can serve with a team in your church. At Christ Fellowship Stuart Campus, our teams have a mantra: *Those who sweat together stick together*. That's called belonging to something bigger than yourself. That speaks of doing something greater than you can do alone. But it takes you getting with some positive people who are doing some positive things. I promise you it will widen your perspective.

Blurred Vision

Your vision is blurred when you are driving too fast. One of the big distractors that keeps you from seeing a wider perspective is you are moving too fast. You are a workaholic. You have too much noise going on. Too much social media. Too much tv. You never stop. A fast life creates a dangerous life. You need to stop a few times every day to be slow and silent. Your perspective is distorted, and you cannot adequately make out what is really going on in your life. You think the problem is people or pressure. It may be a wound deep inside you that you have not given adequate time and space to address. When your vision is blurred, your life will never have clarity.

> A fast life creates a dangerous life.

Proper Place

I am not saying to ignore your struggle. I am certainly not minimizing the pain and devastation it has caused. This is not as simple as out of sight, out of mind. I know the struggle is real, and it is big. So was Goliath to David. So was the wall of Jericho to Joshua. But the key is to put your struggle in its proper place.

We are talking about a healthy perspective. Now, let's stand in the proper place so we can see a proper perspective. It's all where you stand in the scene. It's all about getting the right vantage point. When you are standing in the proper place, the struggle takes on a different meaning. Don't let the struggle stand over you. See it as a trial set before you.

> # Don't let the struggle stand over you. See it as the trial set *before* you.

Paul points us to our example, Jesus Christ, on whom we are to fix our eyes on. His life inspires us. His power fills us. Jesus did not allow His struggle to weigh Him down. He saw His struggle set before Him as the trial that He would have to endure and blow through to cross the finish line. Jesus would overcome. He would push through. He would keep running, keep plowing until He endured all that was necessary to overcome.

When we see the struggle as never-ending, it becomes all-powerful. Your struggle is not all-powerful. It does not have to be never-ending. It is a trial that stands between you and your destiny. Think of this perspective:

THE BIGGER YOUR STRUGGLE, THE GREATER YOUR DESTINY

The struggle is really a trial testing you and developing you for your next level! You are close to graduating, my friend. You are up for a promotion. Trials before you predict promotions in front of you!

Part of a wide perspective is seeing not just where you are, but where you are going. The reason the scripture in Hebrews 12 uses the description of Jesus' struggle as "the joy set before Him", is that Jesus had the perspective of the prize. The struggle foretold of the prize Jesus would achieve. Do you think Jesus thought the cross would be joyful? I don't think so. Do you think Jesus liked pain? No way. In fact, we see in the Bible a time when Jesus was struggling with His struggle. Yes, believe it or not, Jesus was praying for God to remove His struggle!

> Jesus went out as usual to the Mount of Olives, and his disciples followed him. On reaching the place, he said to them, "Pray that you will not fall into temptation." He withdrew about a stone's throw beyond them, knelt down and prayed, "Father, if you are willing, take this cup from me; yet not my will, but yours be done." An angel from heaven appeared to him and strengthened him. And being in anguish, he prayed more earnestly, and his sweat was like drops of blood falling to the ground.
> Luke 22:39-44 NIV

Jesus' prayer is similar to Paul's prayer, in that He is asking God to take away the struggle. Yet, Jesus' prayer is different. Jesus, being fully God, and not just a man, knew all things. He knew that the struggle came with pain and shame. It would mean isolation from His Heavenly Father. Interesting that even with knowing the end from the beginning, Jesus still struggled with His struggle.

That ought to reassure us of two things: First, we can be serving God and still deal with a struggle. Second, we can ask God for help and relief when we feel overwhelmed. Our struggle is real. It is heavy. And God will send Angels to help us endure.

I love how Jesus submitted His will to His Heavenly Father. He did not go by feeling. He lived by faith.
He made a conscious decision that He would not cower in fear. Rather, He would completely trust in God.

Fill Space With Faith

When you see a gap between where you are currently, and how far you have to go, that creates a huge space. When you see how deep and dangerous that chasm is, fill that space with faith in God.

When you cannot see a way forward in the natural, faith sees a way in the supernatural. Faith is walking blind. Faith is listening to the Word of God and stepping in that direction, wherever it leads.

When you begin to step out in faith, your perspective begins to widen. God takes you to a new place where you have never stepped before. Your vantage point broadens so that you can suddenly view so much more.

Faith Widens Your Perspective

Jesus was struggling with His path to the cross. But it was His unflinching faith in God that gave Him the confidence to step forward toward His struggle. The worst part of confronting the struggle usually is just before the pain starts. When you are courageous enough to take that first step in faith to confront your struggle, you will find, like Jesus did, that God will strengthen you. God has victory waiting on the other side for you. God will never leave you nor forsake you.

Victory is what filled Jesus with joy on the front side of his struggle. Hebrews chapter 12 says "for the joy set before Him." The joy was not the pain and shame. It was not being isolated from God. It was not the rejection. No. No sane person enjoys pain!

Jesus had His reward in view. He would conquer the power and evil work of Satan. He would fulfill the sacrifice for sin for all people for all time. Jesus would snatch the keys of hell and rob the grave of death, bringing new life. When Jesus said His final words "it is finished," I believe Jesus smiled with contentment, just as a great champion wins the game.

Maturity is demonstrated by our ability to delay gratification. Jesus had delayed the feeling of accomplishment for 33 years on the earth. Jesus took no short cuts. He fulfilled prophecy and paid the necessary price. This is why the Holy Angels in Heaven sing the song:

> Worthy is the Lamb that was slain, to receive glory and honor, power and dominion forever and ever!
> Revelation 5:12

God's plan for you is to be victorious. He has destined you to win the game. He has made you as champion material. Your future has glory and honor, power and dominion in it! Just like Jesus, you can actually find victory on the other side of your struggle. The key is *what* you focus on. Don't focus on the pain in front of you. Focus on the joy set before you.

> **Don't focus on the pain in front of you.**
> **Focus on the joy set before you.**

Conclusion

It "pains me" to introduce this next chapter to you. This chapter is about pain.

While we should not focus on the pain (it hurts too bad), we need to see that pain can actually help us in overcoming our struggle. I bet you have never considered pain as helpful.

Let me show you.

Chapter 4

The Power of Pain

Pain has a powerful effect. Pain gets our attention. Quickly.

Ever twist your ankle? Ouch!

All of a sudden what you were doing at that moment stops. You are forced to stop dead in your tracks. You are huddled over on the ground in pain. Piercing pain. Excruciating pain. And because I am a baby, I yell and moan. I don't care who hears me. I let it all out. Hello. I am in pain, people!

We try to avoid pain. Naturally, we do not want to feel the powerful effects in our bodies that pain produces. Bad decisions can result in pain. Wrong thinking and wrong living can result in pain. The very nature of pain is that it captures our attention immediately. Pain is very much like a protective mechanism in our lives. It is a warning signal keeping us from destructive behavior.

For some of us, we do not need painful experiences to protect us. We observe warning signs that steer us away from imminent danger. When we drive on the highway and observe the speed limit sign, we heed the speed limit stated on the sign, displaying in big letters 70 MPH. We know the state has set these speed limits to keep the roads relatively safe for all drivers. But for others of us (myself included), we can simply ignore the signs and keep driving how we want. It may not be that we are rebellious or uncaring. It may be that we are running late for our appointment. It may be that we are trying to multi-task our responsibilities by handling business on our cell phone while driving to our destination. For us, we may be in danger of hearing sirens blaring behind us. Uh-oh.

Pain Signals

If you get pulled over by a highway patrolman, it is not a good day. You are probably looking at getting a big, fat speeding ticket. All of a sudden, your biggest problem is not that you are running late. Your bigger problem just became an unexpected payment to the state of $250, money that you did not have planned in your budget.

A speeding ticket is painful. And hearing the warning of the patrol officer telling you that your speeding is dangerous does not feel good either, to say the least. On the outside, you are saying yes and nodding your head as he explains how you broke the law. On the inside, you are hiding how frustrated you are with this officer who just ruined your day and won't give you a break.

As painful as this experience is, you know that the officer is not to blame. You are. You saw the speed limit sign. You know the law. You remember that you have a responsibility when you have a driver's license to abide by the law of the state and drive safely. The officer is not only right in giving you a ticket, he is doing you a favor. Say what??

Speeding tickets are painful, which makes them effective. Nothing hurts us worse than getting tagged with a costly fine. And being corrected by a patrol officer feels humiliating. I know that every time I have been pulled over and been given a speeding ticket, it made me commit to slowing down and mind the laws of driving. It did the trick alright. I have not received tickets in years, because the experience was so painful, so aggravating. It worked.

Now, when I see speed limit signs, I mind the signals. I don't need to go through the pain of getting another speeding ticket. The signal is enough to slow me down. Pain is a powerful signal.

The patrol officer is trying to protect you. You see, the patrol officer deals with car accidents all the time. He has to drive up to the scene of people badly injured or even killed. They see greater pain and destruction. We don't see it like they see it. We don't have to clean up the mess on the road. We don't have to call the families of those who were needlessly killed. We don't feel the pain that the patrol officer feels. The patrol officer is trying to keep this from happening to you. He will make you feel pain so that you don't have to feel pain.

Here is what I want to show you about your struggle. Your struggle is causing you pain, and that is a good thing for you. Yes. It is, actually. Your struggle is signaling that you are in a destructive cycle. You have a habit that is hurting you. And every time you repeat your bad behavior, it creates pain. Over time, the intensity of the pain increases the longer you practice your destructive habits.

The reason I believe God is allowing the struggle to remain in your life is to signal you. The pain you experience points right to the sin or struggle you are dealing with. God loves you so much. He wants to heal you and strengthen you, not harm you. But He knows that if you keep going down this path of destruction, it will eventually kill you. Sin leads to death:

The wages of sin is death.
Romans 6:23

That verse draws a powerful picture of your struggle. The "wages of sin" comes across almost as sarcastic. It is insinuating that all of your work should be producing great income, as a job would award you a paycheck. Payment for services rendered. But when we practice unhealthy habits repeatedly, the "paycheck" is awful. There is a payment for our decisions. Cause and effect. Decisions result in consequences. The path of sin leads to destruction. Your struggle, if left unchecked will lead you down a road that will be death to your dreams. Death to your marriage. Death to your reputation. Death to your potential. Death to your relationships. You will see destruction in your finances, destruction in your body. And sin will eventually take your life, both your body and, more importantly, your soul.

Pain Moves Us

Pain is so powerful, that it has the effect of making us move. When we are experiencing pain, we can't stay where we are.

I love the Disney movie, Lion King. My favorite character is not Simba, who is the Lion King's main character. Rather, I like the baboon, Rafiki. He is the goofy, dancing old sage who becomes a mentor to young Simba. When Simba is in hiding and struggling with his identity, Rafiki jolts him back in to shape. The catalytic moment in the movie is when Rafiki reminds Simba of his calling and purpose. When Simba continues doubting himself, Rafiki uses pain as a lesson.

Simba was doubting himself and was stuck in his struggle to become what he was destined to be. Right as Simba is speaking doubt, Rafiki takes his wooden staff and whacks Simba on the head. Simba says "ouch! What was that for?" Rafiki responds "it doesn't matter. It's in the past." Moments later as Rafiki is teaching his young student, he tests Simba by swinging his staff again to whack his head. This time, Simba ducks from the staff. To avoid the pain of the staff, Simba had to move. Simba had learned a valuable lesson. You can avoid pain when you move away from your destructive position.

I love the story of an old hound dog and his master sitting together on the front porch one morning. A passerby walked by the porch and heard the hound dog howling and moaning. While the dog was howling, the master sat calmly, drinking his coffee looking on. The passerby felt bad for the hound dog and could not believe that the master was not concerned about his dog struggling in his pain and agony. Finally, after hearing the dog howl over and over, the passerby asked the master sitting up on the porch "sir, what is wrong with your dog? He is howling like he is in pain." The master looked at his dog, then took a sip of coffee and responded: "oh, he's just sitting on a nail." The passerby, growing concerned said, "why does the dog not move to another spot on the porch?" The master said, "because it does not hurt enough to move."

How much does your struggle hurt? How much pain is it causing you? On a scale of 1 to 10, what number would you give your pain?

You see, until the pain gets unbearable, you will not so easily move away from your struggle. Understand that if you keep living in your struggle, the pain you experience will become more severe. Let me ask you a question: *how much pain do you need to experience before you are willing to move off of the nail?* That nail is causing you a sharp pain, but you keep sitting on it. Let that pain move you to a place of health. Let that pain force a change in your position. You don't have to feel that pain anymore. It is up to you to move away from the pain.

Refrain from Blame

Most people's reaction to their pain is that they make excuses. They blame others. The pain causes them to moan and groan. The pain is too great for them to bear, and so their knee-jerk reaction is to deflect the true cause of their pain and project it on to others.

Lawyers stay in business because of the pain and suffering that people experience. Slip and fall lawyers advertise that you can make money when you sue someone for causing your pain and suffering. If you can prove somehow that some other person or some business had any part in you experiencing pain, they are responsible. Consequently, they must pay you damages.

Wow. The legal language here is remarkable to me. **YOUR** pain causes damage – *TO YOU*. But the legal system says that you can blame *SOMEONE ELSE* for **YOUR** pain. You can make *SOMEONE ELSE* pay for the damage that you experienced!

While today's society may let you get away with projected blame and excuses, it does not help your situation. Actually, it makes it worse.

> The longer you let the struggle in your life go unchecked, the stronger it grows.

The longer you let the struggle in your life go unchecked, the stronger it grows. The pain that results is so hard to bear, that we do not want to face the truth as to what is the cause of the pain. To feel better, we indulge excuses and blame. Living in a society where our rights are celebrated, we think we are going to address the pain by pointing to outside circumstances happening to us. We think that by identifying people that are causing our pain, the pain will go away. But the only way your pain will actually go away is to do the *painful* work of looking inward. To do this, it will take you to being completely vulnerable. Only when we open up and expose our struggle can we point to the brokenness and weakness in our life.

It takes real courage and maturity to refrain from blame. It takes being objective. It takes letting your defenses down and not allowing any excuses. A mature person takes full responsibility for their life. They do not use outside conditions as a crutch to lean on. When you and I begin to do the difficult work of unpacking our struggle, we must refrain from blame. Become an owner of your struggle. Face your struggle head-on. Confront it. Dig deep in the wound and look at it, as ugly as it is.

Suffering

Suffering is a lost concept. I love our country. Very much. I appreciate our American heritage and I celebrate our founding principles. But one concern that I have for our country is that there is a pervasive mindset in today's generation that people should expect prosperity all of the time. People want to be happy and seek comfort in their everyday lives. There is a goal of working hard Monday through Friday so they can then party and enjoy life.

I love to enjoy life. I am all for working hard and enjoying the rewards of that effort. But the danger of having a goal of prosperity and comfort is that it diminishes the necessity of doing what is necessary to have a healthy, full life. Anybody who has ever reached success and significance understands that suffering is a part of the journey. In fact, they would celebrate their suffering.

Celebrate Your Suffering

No one likes to suffer. Including me. I am NOT, I repeat NOT a glutton for punishment. My friends know I like to chill at Starbucks, or hang out on the couch. The challenge with much of today's generation in America is that they do not want to launch into life. They are fearful of the cost of doing what it takes to acquire what their parents currently possess. They want it now. They almost expect it, as if it is their right as an American. They are used to living in luxury homes and driving in luxury cars. They do not know what it is like not to have a smartphone and wifi service in their home. Flat-screen TVs and Netflix accounts are standard features in every bedroom.

When young people begin to see what a beginner's job opportunity pays, and then look at the cost of the luxury items that they are accustomed to, they become stalled in their pursuit of their life's dreams. And, it's partly not their fault. We, their parents have conditioned them. In an effort to love them and bless them with convenience and comfort, we have actually weakened them. Comfort, while feeling really good, a strong person, does not make.

Suffering is a lost art. Suffering is a powerful tool that can fast-track a person from weakness to strength. Suffering can bring out the greatness and potential of someone. Suffering is no fun. But it produces maturity, confidence, and toughness that prepares a person to tackle life's challenges and overcome.

No discipline seems pleasant at the time, but painful. Later on, however, it produces a harvest of righteousness and peace for those who have been trained by it.
Therefore, strengthen your feeble arms and weak knees. Make level paths for your feet, so that the lame may not be disabled, but rather healed.
Hebrews 12:11-13 NIV

One Way or Another

I like to think of it this way. One way or another, we are
going to experience suffering. One way or another, we will
have to go through a painful process. There is no getting
around the process that life requires. We will mature. We
will learn about ourselves, one way or another. Pay now.
Play later. Or, play now and pay later.

Most of us have to learn the hard way. We don't want to
listen to wisdom given to us by our parents or teachers. We
may have heard that there is this book somewhere in the
Bible that talks about wisdom, but we have never cared to
find a Bible to look it up. (the book is called Proverbs, by
the way. It's worth your time to read. I'm just saying...)

Most of us don't want to listen to any authority figures in
our life. When someone in authority puts restrictions and
rules on us, we feel pushed around. We want freedom. We
don't want to be told what to do. After all, who are they to
tell us how to live? They aren't perfect! They have made
mistakes in their own life.

Whether they are less than perfect is not the issue. Your
parents, your teachers, your coaches, your pastors, your
government leaders are installed by God. They are put
there in your life to test and see if you are willing to listen
and learn. Authority is put in place to protect you from
danger. These people are there to give you oversight
and insight, from their own lessons. When you willingly
submit to authority, you immediately set yourself up to go
farther faster. You bypass all of the painful consequences
of stupidity. Listening to wisdom and correction from
authorities puts you ahead of others in the line to success.

But, unfortunately, most of us have to learn the hard
way. We can't take their word for it. We have a spirit of

rebellion. This spirit opposes God and His laws. The Bible calls it witchcraft:

> For rebellion is as the sin of witchcraft, and stubbornness is as iniquity and idolatry. Because thou hast rejected the word of the Lord,
> 1 Samuel 15:23 KJV

In the Bible, rebellion happened all the time. We see God, the Father, and His children, the people of Israel at odds. This sounds funny as I write it, because no one can stand at odds with the Creator of Heaven and Earth. But the newly freed Hebrew slaves are fresh out of Egypt and they have soon forgotten how bad they had it in their 400-year struggle being tormented by the Egyptian slave masters. God had raised up a savior to deliver them out of slavery and bring them into a beautiful promised land to live in community with God. God had done spectacular signs and wonders in Egypt right before their eyes, to prove to both the Hebrews and the Egyptians that God was indeed the great I AM.

Even after God parted the Red Sea to create a path of escape for His children, they doubted Him. Even after destroying the impending Egyptian army behind them, they continued to question God's Word. Even after God provided food and provisions, having given them the wealth from their Egyptian taskmasters, God's children fought against His plan.

When Moses, the leader whom God appointed, led God's Children to the land of Canaan to take it as their own, the people doubted and rebelled. The people questioned Moses' leadership. The people actually had the audacity to suggest that they had life better in Egypt. In slavery!

Because of the children's response, God told Moses they would wander the desert for 40 years. 40 is a significant number in the Bible, mentioned 146 times. The number means a time of trial or testing. God had previously tested the children of Israel by leading them in the wilderness for 40 days while 12 of them were scouting out the land of Canaan. Because of Israel's response of doubt and rebellion against Moses, God would now extend the testing time from days to years. Living in the desert traveling all of the time was tough. It was a time of suffering. And to wander the desert for 40 years meant that the elders living now among Israel would not live to see the Promised Land.

This story is worth reading for yourself in the Bible, Numbers Chapters 13 and 14. God had planned to fast-track His children from slavery to success. From pain to promise. 40 days of listening, trusting and obeying would have put the children of Israel in a beautiful land flowing with milk and honey. Now, they would learn the lesson the hard way, wandering the desert for 40 years. One way or another, God would do what He must to mature and teach His beloved Children. What could have taken days to learn would now take years.

What could have taken days to learn would now take years.

When we obey what God says, it requires some suffering. God's ways are not the world's ways. God's ways point to holiness. They point to truth and righteousness. Righteousness means living right according to what God says is right.

Let's focus this back to your struggle. When you do the hard work of installing discipline in your life, you will experience some suffering. Hebrews Chapter 12 says that no discipline seems good at the time. Discipline means restricting yourself. It means telling yourself no. And, it means inviting authority figures in your life, letting them give you direction.

When you were a child, you had parents, teachers, and coaches giving you direction and correction. You had no choice to follow their orders. Just because you are older does not mean that you do not need "parents" giving you direction and correction. You and I ABSOLUTELY need authority over our us, now more than ever. More is at stake. If you have responsibility for people and resources, more is expected of you. More could go wrong. If you fall, others will fall. You and I need accountability!

So, the choice is yours. The question isn't if you will experience suffering. The question is actually when. When do you want to go through it? Now? Or Later?

If you listen to wisdom by your authority figure, you will choose now. You will start today. No excuses. No blame. You will choose to embrace the pain now. It will suck. It will hurt. You will get your ego bruised. You will not agree with everything asked of you. But, if you choose now, your suffering will be short. It could be 3 months, or 3 years. Depending on the struggle you are dealing with, the journey is uphill, all the way. No shortcuts. No magic carpet ride. Don't look back to Egypt. Look ahead. It takes focus, courage, and humility. And you will suffer.

If you listen to yourself, and not your authority figure, you are choosing later. Today is just another day of accepting your struggle. Do what feels good now. If you listen to yourself, you begin making excuses. You blame people who hurt you. You blame your coaches for being demanding. You blame God and accuse Him for judging you and not taking this struggle away from you. Your suffering will grow over time, becoming more painful. Your life will become smaller, more isolated. People don't want to be with someone who is small and weak. That is depressing. Your life will get small as your struggle becomes great. Soon, people will identify you not by your dream, but by your struggle. I wish I could say that your suffering will end in a given time, but I can't. You struggle will rule your life. There will be no end to your suffering. This is tragedy.

One way or another, you will suffer. Embrace the suffering. Lean in to the "suck". The sooner you start, the more you will begin to realize that the uphill climb is not as awful as you might have thought. And when you trust that the pain and suffering are actually moving you toward a place of health and freedom, you can better embrace the pain.

For our light and momentary troubles are achieving for us an eternal glory that far outweighs them all.
2 Corinthians 4:17 NIV

When you are learning patterns of health and righteous living, they will feel painful at first. They will feel restrictive. Not everybody practices spiritual and physical disciplines, so you will feel alone. The Apostle Paul, who wrote from his own uphill climb experience, gives us a great mindset when we are going through the suffering to overcome our struggle. Think of the pain and suffering as "light and momentary."

How we think is important. Vital, actually. If our struggle has had a hold on us, we need to take that power away from our struggle. We are more powerful than we think. We have the potential for greatness. We were designed to be victorious. We have a God-given purpose and have been fashioned with God-given gifts. We have God-given insight and creativity. We have not yet realized our strength and health. We have not yet fulfilled our potential. We have been living down there, not up here.

When you and I begin to see our suffering as "light and momentary", it gives us hope. It builds momentum. We are going somewhere. We are moving forward. Our suffering is producing strength and muscles in our life, both physically and spiritually. When bodybuilders start gaining muscle successfully, they learn to embrace the pain and suffering that their bodies go through. They actually ENJOY the pain. It becomes a high for them. The "pump" is the term bodybuilders use to describe the feeling of pain that gives them that high. The high comes from the thought that they are growing stronger. Their suffering *strengthens* their struggle.

Conclusion

Every time you feel restricted, every time you feel corrected by your authority figure, *feel the "pump"*. When you have to resist temptation, when you have to make the right choice, even when it is not the fun choice, *feel the pain*. Realize that you are building strength. You are building muscles. Pain is powerful. Learn to use it to your advantage. Growth does not come without pain. Don't let pain happen to you. Embrace the power of pain and see great gains.

In this next chapter, I want to start getting into the *how-to* in mastering your struggle. While tough at first, you will learn how to build a system that can sustain your growth in the area of your struggle. Whether your struggle is a sin, a weakness, or a bad habit, this process has helped me overcome some areas in my life. Maybe your struggle is dealing with some pain or abuse that happened to you, but now has a hold over you. A struggle is a difficulty that keeps you down. Or, it is an opposition that is keeping you from moving forward toward your life's purpose.

Working on struggles that prove difficult or that oppose us are ongoing. I have struggles in my life that I still am working to master. Before we become a master, we must start as a student. Let's be students now...together.

Chapter 5

Mastering Your Struggle

I love war movies. Most guys do.

Guys are drawn to conflicts and contests. They are inspired by courage and valor. Good versus evil stuff. My wife wants me to watch "sweet" movies with her. While I love spending time together with my wife, I have made it clear to Kellie that I am NOT going to be sitting and watching a "sweet" movie. Sweet makes me *sick*.

What I think is "sweet" is when the bad guys are getting pummeled in a bloody battle. There is something about seeing an underdog good guy having to overcome insurmountable odds to fight against a dark, powerful enemy that inspires me. Consequently, battles and conflicts make my sweet wife sick. Go figure.

One of my favorite battle movies is The 13th Warrior, starring Antonio Banderas. It is an epic tale staged in the age of the fabled Viking era. This movie has all the guts and glory a red-blooded man could hope for. Let me set it up for you...

A mythical darkness has fallen on the land of Scandinavia. The Norse People are living in fear of a strange race of creatures who live in the caves of nearby mountains. These half-human, half bear creatures are called Eaters of the Dead. They would eat their victims.

The Norse People, seeking a solution to their struggle, looked to an elderly woman. She is the Ancient Seer in the village, giving the people spiritual direction. She prophecies that 13 valiant men would find the Eaters of the Dead and destroy them. She hand-selects 12 of the strongest, seasoned Vikings in the village to go. Yet, one warrior was yet to be identified.

In the village, there was a foreigner from Arabia who had stumbled into their village. He was a poet who had been banished from the court of the Sultan in Baghdad. He was watching the selection process happen from the back of the room when the elderly woman pointed right at him. Everyone looked around wondering if she was mistaken. She kept pointing at this short foreigner. She was clearly selecting him as the 13th and final warrior to join the mission.

The 12 Viking Warriors laughed at him. He had never been in a battle before. He rode a short Arabian horse. He had a small sword. Yet, he had timidly accepted the challenge and followed the other warriors up the mountain to hunt down the enemy.

As they were preparing for battle, one of the Vikings started to help the poet. The Viking took away the poet's small sword and gave him a larger weapon, one that the warriors carried. "Use this" he instructed. The Arabian poet tried to swing it, but could not control it. "It's too heavy. I cannot use this!" he cried out.

The Viking looked back at him and challenged: "grow stronger."

Throughout the movie, we follow the metamorphosis of this nervous, weak poet becoming a brave warrior. He learns the Norse language. He sharpens his skills and studies the enemy. It is this 13th Warrior that identifies the half-human, half bears as just normal people who dress like Bears to intimidate their enemies. They can be killed like any man.

The 13 Warriors battle and finally conquer the Eaters of the Dead. But the greatest victory is that the once weak poet becomes a warrior.

Learn to Fight

There is something to be learned in this story. While the Arabian Poet found himself faced with a struggle of being chosen for a task too great for him, he did not cower in fear. He did not stay small. Instead, he embraced the challenge of his fellow Viking Warrior and started to figure out how to overcome it. The poet became a warrior, and the warrior won the day. The poet observed the Vikings, learned from them and began to work on the fighting skills and the language so that he could become a master. Once he became a master in fighting skills, in strategy and in language, the other Viking Warriors would afford him respect and would lean on him to fight alongside them.

> The weak becomes the warrior.

We need to become a master over our struggle. We need to rule over it. Just learning to live with it is not an option. That won't allow us to move forward to what God has called us to. We must learn skills and enact practices that will move from weakness to warrior.

Grow Stronger

The secret to overcoming your struggle is...get stronger. Grow stronger. Ask yourself:

What will it take for me to grow stronger?

What do I have to do to build the muscles to overcome this struggle in my life?"

The Apostle Paul was hoping God would remove his struggle. Paul was looking for the easy button. A quick fix. But God pushed Paul into a process of growth. There is no cheating the process. You can't sidestep it. You can't rush through it. You have to start with day one. Then, get up the next morning and start on day two. The sooner you embrace the process, the sooner you get on your way to strength.

In the book, Created to Crave, a Navy Seal shares his perspective of the work ethic and intensity that Navy Seals possess. I loved this quote when I read it and just had to include it in this chapter:

WE SWEAT HARD IN PREPARATION SO WE DON'T BLEED IN BATTLE.

Growing stronger takes sweat equity. It takes an intensity and an aggressive mindset to do the work necessary to get to a higher level. Staying the same requires only that you keep doing what you're doing. Nothing more. Nothing less. But to build bigger muscles, you have to use heavier weights.

We've all heard the adage, *to get somewhere you have never been, you are going to have to do something that you have never done.* If you have not heard that before, you need to. That will help you. Most of us see a challenge and start trudging forward just doing more of what we are doing now. More panicking, more busyness, more struggling. All that gets us is nowhere fast, like spinning our wheels in a ditch. Giving it more gas just spins your wheels faster. That just throws mud everywhere.

To grow stronger, you are going to need to begin to open your mind. Wide. You are going to need to start thinking differently. New thoughts. New concepts. You need to become a learner. I want to urge you to lay down your pretense and your pride. Humble yourself and become a level-one learner. Start from scratch. Listen with a blank slate. I am going to help you learn how to grow stronger. I have done it in my life in several areas, and I have found success. Great success. Listen to me. Are you willing to listen? Do I have your attention? Here we go.

Space

Most of us like our space. I like mine. Leave me alone. Give me my space. Don't tell me what to do. One common compliant I hear from people: don't micro-manage me.

Space is great when we know what to do with it. When we know how to use it effectively in our life, space affords us great liberty to think, create, take risk, and experiment. I love space. I don't like to be forced to follow someone else's map, someone else's guidelines. Even if they are right, I still like to explore and discover. That's just how I am wired.

The problem with space is that most of us abuse the space we are given. If we are given freedom in our schedule, we waste time. If we are given space on how to lead a project at work, we don't use wisdom and planning to ensure that the project is successful. We don't prepare like we should. We don't study like we should. We don't work intentionally on the right work. And when the project fails, we are left with disappointment.

If you were honest enough to look at the struggle in your life on a chart and evaluate how it grew, you would learn a lot. If you could point to some key events that happened to you, and notice some opportunities missed and choices made, you would slowly begin to piece together a clear diagnosis of why you struggle the way you do. What you may soon realize is that you had too much free space for missed opportunities and poor choices which led to your struggle growing as big as it has become.

Struggle Needs Structure

When we struggle, we need structure. We need structure in our lives to help us deal with our struggle in a healthy way. While our tendency may be to view structure as rigid or restraining, we ought to view it more as life-giving.

A structure is necessary for growth. Well, let me be more specific. A structure is necessary to shape a particular type of growth that you desire. Landscapers understand this principle when they use a trellis to grow plants. They will plant a vine-like plant in the ground, and then set up a structure near it called a trellis. As the plant begins to grow, they will wrap the vines on to the trellis, guiding it  through the structure. It takes time for the plant to fully mature before the trellis is covered with the vines. Slowly, as the designer prunes away vines that do not align with the trellis, and even prunes the vines that are healthy and reaching upward, the trellis transforms from an empty wooden structure to a full bloom spectacle that everyone who views it appreciates.

The word, trellis originates from the Greek language, meaning "rule." A rule demands a certain direction be followed. A rule restricts any direction or behavior, other than the clear intention designed. While rules do not inspire passion or enthusiasm, they do enable growth by design. Rules force growth to move in a certain direction. Rules allow growth to build and rise higher than just allowing growth to happen naturally.

I appreciate beautiful landscape. Living in South Florida affords me a climate that promotes tropical plants. One of my favorite plants is the bougainvillea. It blooms bright colors, which give a home an accent for curb appeal. I love when I can spot a bougainvillea in a neighborhood. The brilliant color pops out at me.

Years ago, my wife and I bought a bougainvillea plant and put it in a pot in front of our driveway. I wanted our house to pop with that pink bloom. However, after a few months of watering and fertilizing, the plant would not bloom as I had hoped. And, it was not growing tall along the front entrance of my home. It seemed that my neighbor's bougainvillea was always in full bloom and was growing tall and beautiful. What about mine?

I learned that the plant did not need as much water as I was giving it (I was drowning it.) It needed more fertilizer. Also, it would not grow bigger in a pot. I needed to plant it in the ground so that the roots could go down deeper and extend. And lastly, I needed to buy a trellis and train the vines around it. This was a lot of work! I am impatient, and I grew tired of having to manage the growth of this plant. Once I planted my bougainvillea in the ground, it grew huge! I could not keep up with the pruning. I would always get poked by the spikes – ouch! The good news was that it was growing bigger and was starting to bloom. The hard part was twisting those heavy, spiky vines around the trellis. That was a task! I ended up removing the bougainvillea from my front yard. Too much work getting the bougainvillea to follow the direction of the trellis.

Following rules is hard work. It takes daily adherence to following guidelines that will train you up to where you want to grow to. Your tendency will be to do what feels right, what looks good in the moment. Your emotions will scream at you to not follow the rules. Your mind will play tricks on you, talking you out of the discipline you know you should follow.

What Are You Allowing to Grow?

You see, growth happens. Something *is* going to grow in your life. When there is life, there is growth. The question is, what are you allowing to grow? Something is going to grow naturally. You don't have to make it grow. It just grows on its own. Just like my bougainvillea plant, your life will grow big when given space. The problem is that if you don't control what grows, you are going to have a huge, overgrown plant in your life growing in every direction. If left unattended, it will have become so massive, that it spills over to the rest of your life. My bougainvillea would grow so wide, that I could hardly park my car in my driveway because the spikey

> Left un-attended, bad habits become big struggles.

vines had encroached beyond the house. Getting out of my car, I would get poked! Now, you can see why I finally had enough and got rid of that plant?!

Something has been growing in you. Left unattended, bad habits become big struggles. Without the training of rules, your thoughts become attitudes. Your emotions becomes strongholds. Without the proper healing and proper exercises, a wound becomes a permanent mark that defines you. What happened TO you has BECOME who you are.

The power of a structure is that it *forces* your growth in a certain direction. Structure puts rules in place that you must follow. A trellis is a structure that rules your thoughts, your emotions, and your actions. You no longer have to make tough decisions throughout the day on what is best. You are simply following the rules. The rules tell you what to do, where to go, what to think.

You are no longer in charge. Your rules are in charge.

They direct. You follow.

They dictate. You align.

Simple.

By creating structure, you become the master-designer of your life. You get to decide what the rules are. You get to build the trellis for your life. The structure can be fashioned exactly the way you need it to be so that you can get what you want in life. You can grow in the direction you want to go. This is such an effective mindset tool for you. You see, on the front end, when you are rested, stable, and objective, you can decide on what you want to grow to. You can design your structure. You can designate the rules you will follow. Once you have committed to this, then you willingly submit yourself to the rules you have designed. When you are tired, frustrated, discouraged, or hurt, that is when you simply follow the rules. You adhere to the structure set. No deciding. No compromising. No excuses. Simply follow.

Learning this design tool of a structure now empowers you to be intentional about what you choose to grow in your life. Do you want to be physically healthy? Then design a structure to build that. Simply follow the rules you set.

Do you want to beat an addiction? There are effective structures already designed that are proven to help you overcome in the area you struggle in. Celebrate Recovery is an excellent program that churches across America offer. Look it up and get into a group today.

Do you want to get out of debt? Tired of being stressed about not having enough money? Dave Ramsey built a structure for that. He built it from overcoming his own financial struggle. Now, he is helping people all over America. Look up Financial Peace University. Simply follow his rules, which he calls "Baby Steps".

Whatever your struggle is, a structure has been built or can be custom-built to help you overcome. You can find freedom. You can see healthy growth, intentional growth that you dream of. Follow the rules, don't follow your emotions or thoughts. *Don't trust yourself, trust the structure.*

You Need a Parent

When we are children, we must follow the directions of our parents. If you were blessed to have good parents, they would love you, but also restrict you. Parents had rules:

- Must be in bed by 8 PM.
- Eat your vegetables.
- No cursing.
- Take a bath.
- Don't hit your sister.
- Be respectful to the teacher.
- You will go to church with our family.
- Do your chores, because we all pitch in at home.

Children will question rules. *"Why do I have to do this?"* The parents will say *"because I said so."* Children usually hate rules. They try to get out of doing what they are asked. They are **unruly**. But a good parent will enforce the rules by creating consequences. Punishment will be given when the rules are not followed. Of course, children feel mistreated when they are punished. Cell phones are taken away. They have to do extra chores at home. If the child had been disrespectful to a teacher, the parent makes them apologize. But the child has no choice. They live in their parent's home, and they must follow the parent's rules. The parents **rule** over the children.

So let me pose this thought to you. Now that you are grown, do you think you no longer need to follow rules? Do you think that because you are over 21 years of age, you don't need to answer to anybody?

On the contrary, I am advocating that you DO need a parent – more than ever. You need rules dictating and directing your life now more than you needed them when you were a child in your parent's home. You see, when you were a child, your parents were there to protect you, restrain you and correct you. You did not have to think for yourself. They did that for you.

Now that you are out of the house, grown and in charge, no one is thinking for you. No one can control you. You have freedom. You have rights. You have a choice. Too much space. No one is watching you. Now, more than ever, you need a structure guiding you. You need clear rules that are lines of demarcation that you adhere to. And you need a few people in authority in your life to act as a type of parent over you. You need to be honest with them, sharing your hurts, habits and hang-ups. You need to bring them into a design process of your structure. You need to give them permission to hold you accountable to the rules you know will get you growing intentionally in the right direction. Here is the structure process:

1. Design your life - intentional growth plan

2. Build a structure - schedule healthy habits

3. Define your rules - what I *will* do, what I *will not* do

4. Invite a parent - someone who will reinforce your rules and support your structure

Hey friend, this is no joke. This takes a lot of work. This takes some time to design. There will be times this structure will frustrate you, like growing my bougainvillea plant was frustrating for me. You will poke your finger on the vine trying to get your growth to follow the rule of the trellis, and you will want to just tear the whole plant up out of the ground and be done with it! I know the feeling.

Growing your life intentionally takes patience. Growing your life intentionally flows in an upward direction. It is uphill all the way. If you just let your life grow, it will grow in any direction it wants to. That is when it becomes too much to manage. Just like my bougainvillea was growing into my driveway, you will have bad habits and past hurts overgrowing into other areas of your life. They will show up in your marriage and at work. Your struggle with anxiety or fear will manifest itself physically making you sick. The reason you are overwhelmed with your struggle is because it has become overgrown. It is uncontrollable. It is growing everywhere and anywhere. That is why building a structure is necessary. The structure you submit to will give you great success.

No discipline seems pleasant at the time, but painful. Later on, however, it produces a harvest of righteousness and peace for those who have been trained by it.
Hebrews 12:11 NIV

Struggle needs a structure. When we follow a structure, we eventually reach success. Whether it takes days, months, or even years, your structure is built for your success. You can achieve the growth that you dream about. You can reach the goals that you set out to accomplish. You want to lose 50 pounds? If you follow the structure and let it rule you, it's only a matter of time. The structure likely has some rules built in it restricting sugar and carbs, insisting on defined amounts of water consumed, weight training accompanied by rest periods and healthy sleep. Following a structure of a certain amount of calories allowed daily will eventually get you to your goal of losing 50 pounds. While you may not follow the structure to perfection, if you keep moving forward and push yourself to follow your self-imposed rules, you will see stated progress. Because you are human, you will not always follow perfectly. But following the structure long enough will eventually get you the success you once thought unreachable. Structure enables success.

Your Struggle Becomes Your Story

When you master your struggle, you will have a story to tell. An inspiring one. The journey you have had to traverse has set you in a place of proven experience. What had almost taken you out will now set you up. The struggle that was holding you down will become the story that you will hold up to show the world that you have defeated it!

Just like the Bible character, David held up the head of his foe, Goliath, you hold up your struggle proudly to all who are watching. Your trial becomes your trophy. This is not a moment to stay hidden and humble. This is not a time to keep it to yourself. No! Hold that head high. Shout a blood-curdling cry of victory for all to hear. Shout it loud and long. You are a mighty warrior! With God's help and power, you have defeated your struggle. Stand tall. Chest out. Share your story.

Your story is powerful. Your story is powerful to share with others. It is a powerful tool for *you*. When you realize the significance of the struggle you have faced in your life, you begin to connect it to your life's story. I'm talking about your purpose. Your God-given purpose.

> Your story is powerful.

You see, there is an enemy out there. Satan is real, and he is your enemy. You may not believe in devils or demons, but the Bible shows us they are indeed real.

Satan is against you because he is against God. Whatever God creates, Satan works to destroy. Whatever God loves, Satan hates. Because your Heavenly Father loves you and has created you for a holy purpose, Satan is working against you.

The name, Satan means adversary. It means one who opposes. Satan does not want you to become what God has intended for you. He knows you are weak. He sees your struggle and your sin. With every opportunity, Satan uses your struggle to beat you down and keep you there. As long as you stay down and don't struggle, he will not bother you. It is when you try to struggle to stand up, that his attacks of lies and temptation start pushing you back down.

Young women today are attacked in the area of comparison. The Social Media culture has propagated an allusion that women have to look perfect. Perfect body, perfect skin. Barbie doll is the standard that women believe they must live up to. A flood of images reinforce this lie in the minds and hearts of women, leaving them feeling worthless.

As a Pastor, I have dealt with too many families in our church who are struggling with a daughter who is dabbling in drugs and experimenting with sex. These young ladies are beautiful, inside and out. They are smart, pretty, and have wonderful personalities. Their families are raising them in church, and have built healthy support systems for them to reach their full potential. And yet, parents are bewildered as to why their daughters are cutting themselves, overdosing, and giving themselves sexually to anyone who will take them. What God has designed them to be and purposed for their life, girls are now forfeiting because the world tells them they cannot measure up. So, the world lures them into experimentation and escape.

I am grateful to be the father of a beautiful daughter. Madison is 19 years old. My wife, Kellie and I are SO PROUD of her! She is studying to be a Nurse, a difficult tract to be accepted in to, but she made it with flying colors. Madison is also a gifted singer. She has studied piano since she was 5 years old and has been singing in church since she was 11 years old.

Everyone who sees Madison sing comments on how beautiful she is. They speak of her kindness, her maturity, and her success. Yet, Madison will tell you that she struggles with feelings of fear and insecurity. One would never think it be possible that a young lady as beautiful, successful, and gifted as Madison would struggle! But there are moments when she questions herself and questions her gifting. Usually in seasons of stress and tiredness is when we hear her share her struggle.

Kellie and I are SO GLAD we have a close relationship with our daughter that she feels safe to come to us with her feelings. We have reminded her that there is a special calling God has purposed for her. Satan wants to destroy her life before she even gets started. Satan knows her struggle, and he uses every attack and scheme in today's culture to get her comparing herself and questioning her gift.

Madison's gift of singing is so awesome. So Satan does everything he can to discourage her from doing that. Isn't that just like that awful snake? When Madison sings in our church, so many people come tell me how gifted and special she is. They are inspired by her singing, and even more by her life. She is pure. Humble. Healthy. Going the right way. She is bringing glory to God. Madison's life is revealing the Name of Jesus!

A few years ago, my wife and I had a precious family in our home for dinner. This family serves together with us at Christ Fellowship in Stuart, Florida. As our teenage kids left the dinner table, Kellie and I talked with our dinner guests, David and Rebecca. We shared the challenges we face in raising our children in today's culture. As we shared with David and Rebecca how Madison struggles with her singing, they could not believe what they were hearing. They loved Madison and saw such an anointing of God on her life.

David has a prophetic gift that God has used in his life. He asked me if he could pray over Madison. I agreed and went and brought Madison into the living room. Kellie, Rebecca, David and I all surrounded Madison there in our home as David prayed this scripture verse over her life:

When the enemy comes in like a flood, the Lord will lift up a standard against him.
Isaiah 59:19

David declared:

> Madison, God is raising you up as a standard
> in this culture
>
> You are a standard of holiness
>
> You are a standard of purity
>
> Your life is God's standard to show your
> generation Jesus Christ

That moment marked Madison's life. It marked my life. I come from a line of Christians. Not just Christians, but Pastors. I am a third-generation Pastor. I believe that night, the Holy Spirit fell on our home. That night, His holy presence rested on my daughter, Madison. Through the prayer of a Prophet, God was confirming His favor and purpose on my beautiful daughter. Though she would always have to combat the struggle of significance, she had clearly heard God's voice confirm her calling for special use in ministry. Beautiful!

The enemy attacks your calling

The enemy will attack the area surrounding your calling. If you are called to preach, the enemy will attack your ability to speak up. If you are called to lead, the enemy will attack your confidence. If you are called to sing like Madison, the enemy will make you question your gift. If you are dealing with a struggle, take a moment to ask the question "why am I struggling with this?"

Why am I struggling with weight loss?

Why am I struggling with lust?

Why am I struggling with anxiety?

Why am I struggling with fear?

Why am I struggling with anger?

Why am I struggling with debt?

When you take time to study the trigger points of your struggle, you begin to see a pattern. You will discover that pattern is circling around your calling. Don't believe me? Ask 3 people who know you well. Ask your parents. Ask a teacher you trust. Ask a coach. Get with your pastor or group leader at church. Give them permission to be brutally honest with you. They see it. They will help you see it. Don't talk. Just listen. Take notes. Write out words that pop out. That is insight, hitting you square in the face.

Your struggle will reveal your calling

God many times will not remove your struggle from your life. Like the Apostle Paul, God says "no. My grace is sufficient for you." Like Paul, God is revealing your calling through your struggle. Paul had a calling to reveal Jesus through preaching and teaching. In his early life, he grew up in privilege and education. Paul came from the pedigree of a prominent family. Paul was afforded opportunities to learn from the best Rabbis, studying in the best schools. One coming from such a stature of success could only be left to figure that they had everything they needed to fulfill their calling. However, one step was left remaining. One key piece was necessary for this accomplished, apt pupil.

You see, education cannot replace experience. To reach people who don't have what you have, you must walk where they walk. If you have never had a lack, your plenty will not prepare you. If you have always belonged as an insider, you don't feel the loneliness of the outsider.

God was allowing Paul to learn by experience. Real-time pain and suffering was a prerequisite to his preaching. The struggle Paul asked to be taken, God let remain. Was God deaf? Was He uncaring? Had Satan had his way in Paul's life?

On the contrary. Paul's suffering was a setup. God had called Paul to reveal Jesus, but He was shifting Paul's assignment to another group of people. All of Paul's life, he thought he was preparing to be a Rabbi to his own Jewish people, God's Chosen people. But God's heart was to bring the Gentiles into His family. God's heart was for *whosoever will call upon the name of the Lord*, that they are saved. God's heart was not just to reach His chosen children. His heart extended for His adopted children.

For Paul to know how to reach those on the outside, Paul would have to understand their struggle. It is only when one walks in some else's shoes that they can relate to their journey. Paul, who was comfortable with school, success, and status, would have to learn to be uncomfortable with suffering and struggle.

YOUR SUFFERING IS A SETUP.

How can you teach someone to master their struggle if you have not mastered yours? How can you expect to carry any credibility with your student if you cannot model what you have mastered? Too many teachers out there share a 10-minute video on how easy it is to lose weight. But when they gain the weight back, their video channel grows quiet years later.

Only those strugglers out there who have done the hard work to master their struggle can carry a message worth listening to. Only the warriors bloodied and scarred by their battle can teach from experience how freedom is possible. Their adversity builds them their audience.

God has a calling planted in your life. Right now, it may be hidden. Like a seed planted in the ground, it may be small. No branches sprouting out. No fruit to offer. The seed remains dormant, like a dream. Currently, your struggle dominates. But as you begin to study your struggle, you allow God's calling to begin to be revealed – to you, and to your mentors and inner-circle friends.

Discovering that beautiful seed will inspire you. Like a fresh, morning rain, the Holy Spirit will sprinkle on your seed. As the seed grows, it pushes against your struggle. There is a tension. A pressure building. What will you allow to grow? Your seed? Or your struggle? Both need food. Both need love and care. Both are crying for your attention. Feed me!

Feed Your Seed

As you feed your seed, you will starve your struggle. Don't give energy to resisting your struggle. Give energy rather than growing your seed. This is powerful! Whatever you feed grows.

> Whatever you feed grows.

Control what you look at. Discipline what you think about. Focus on your dream. Remember your calling. Write it down. Say it aloud. Work on your dream. A dream becomes reality when you set deadlines. The structure you have built will set you up for success! Following the rules and not your feelings will move you upward and onward. The people you have invited in your life will cheer you on.

They will support you and remind you of your purpose and your calling.

As you build your dream, your dream becomes bigger. It becomes colorful. More specific. Now you are starting to see life spring up from the ground. It's small. Just a little leaflet. But it is moving upward, reaching for the sky. It is *struggling* to grow. Now your struggle is not with your sin issue. Your struggle becomes making your dream become a reality!

Conclusion

This is exciting stuff. Your calling is a huge motivator for you to master your struggle. Once you achieve mastery, you will need to learn to manage it. Remember that you are in a battle. The enemy is attacking you. And your flesh is weak. Living in your calling is always an uphill fight. This next chapter will teach you how you can live in freedom. The key is good management.

Chapter 6

Managing Your Struggle

"It's not the load that breaks you down. It's the way you carry it." –Coach Lou Holtz

Once we have learned mastery over our struggle, managing becomes much easier. The mastery is the hard work upfront that pays off later.

Think of mastery as pushing a heavy cart uphill. Then think of managing as reaching the top of the hill and then just coasting along even ground. You still have to keep moving forward pushing the cart, but you don't feel the weight of resistance that you once did. The weight that initially felt so heavy now is manageable. Why? Because you have built the muscle mass to handle it. You have learned a technique on how to work more efficiently. With strength, skill, and insight, you will be able to manage your struggle. You can achieve victory over your struggle through learning mastery. But it is learning management that will keep you there.

Does this mean that your struggle will go away? Are you able to take your foot off the gas pedal and just relax? Absolutely not! Please do not misunderstand - managing takes work. It requires giving attention and careful precision on a daily basis. One wrong move and you could slip easily into wrong thinking and bad habits. Don't think for a minute you can forgo all of the structure and the accountability I coached in the previous chapter. Living that out in a disciplined way is how you will manage your life from now on. Doing this will simply reduce the pain and suffering you experienced in learning to master over your struggle.

I want to study a scripture verse with you that deals with this. *Side note: notice how I study scripture by breaking them down, understanding their context and their meaning. This is something I want you to begin to do in your daily routine. I want you to make time to read at least one scripture EVERY DAY. My suggestion is that it be the first thing you do in the morning. God's Word gives you power. God's Word is **God speaking** directly to you. God's Word is life. Starting your morning with reading scripture is the most powerful weapon you can arm yourself with.*

Let's take a look at this text:

> No temptation has overtaken you except what is common to mankind. And God is faithful; he will not let you be tempted beyond what you can bear. But when you are tempted, he will also provide a way out so that you can endure it.
>
> 1 Corinthians 10:13 NIV

No temptation has overtaken you except what is <u>common</u> to mankind.

No struggle is unique. No sin or abuse is unique to your situation. You may feel like you are the only one dealing with this, but you are not. Other people have had the same experiences you have faced.

It helps to realize that you are not alone. You are not weird. Many times what keeps us stuck in a struggle is not knowing exactly what the struggle is. It is like thinking you have something wrong with you physically. You feel it. You sense it. When you go to the doctor for tests, they cannot tell you immediately what it is. They cannot find a diagnosis. The waiting makes us worry.

Only when you get the test results back do you rest easier. Even if it is bad news, you can deal with it. Even if you are dealing with cancer, you can grasp that reality. Now, you can begin to fight it. Knowing what you are dealing with allows you to move forward toward health. Understanding that your struggle is common to man puts handles on it for you to grab hold of. There are resources available for you. There are coaches ready to help you. Other people who struggled like you have found mastery over this same struggle. They can be an inspiration and can offer insight on how they now manage in a healthy way.

And God is faithful; he will not let you be tempted beyond what you can bear.

God will not put you in a spot where you are doomed to fail. No. God is faithful. He is always with you, always watching. God is using your struggle as a heavy weight to build muscles.

Notice here in this text that while it says that God is faithful, God does not save you from the struggle. God does not remove the temptation. He regulates the amount of temptation according to what you can bear. This is a relief. But this is also a forecasting:

If you think you were struggling before you mastered your struggle, *get ready.* When you reach a level of victory in your struggle, guess what? God will challenge you with more temptation – more weight to bear. One Pastor preached this, declaring *new levels, new devils.*

Why does God allow this? Because He is building you up. You are being broken down to be built up in the image of His Son, Jesus. He is pruning you. Refining you. Following Jesus is no easy task. There is a breaking before a building happens. That is Jesus' building process.

When you are managing your struggle successfully, God will bring heavier weights, stronger temptations to keep taking you to the next level. You are in a constant cycle of mastery, manage, mastery, manage...

Mastery	Management
Level 1	Level 1
Level 2	Level 2
Level 3	?
?	?

How far have you come? How far are you willing to go? When you get to level 2 and learn to manage it, it isn't long before God is preparing you for mastery level 3, your next contest. Comfortable feels good, but it does not help build character. Only resistance training can do that. God is more concerned about your character than your comfort.

But when you are tempted, he will also provide a way out so that you can **endure** it."

God is not evil. He is not harsh. Is He tough? Yes. Any loving father is. Just like I was testing my children in the swimming pool, our Heavenly Father is testing us now. But be assured, He will never let you drown. He will never leave you to sink. He will always provide a way out. He may allow you to bend, but He will not cause you to break. You can endure it! Yes you can.

When you are weak, tired and tempted, your emotions tell you that you cannot escape the trap of sin. But the truth of God's Word will rise up within you (...IF you have been reading God's Word every morning...) and reinforce that you can escape and you can endure.

When you are in a management mindset, you simply have to call upon the muscles you have built. You simply rely upon the structure and rules you have set in place. You follow the plan. Take a deep breath, speak God's Word out loud, and start the next day.

I want to give some practical steps that I practice to help me manage my life so that I keep mastery over my struggles. I call these steps my strengthening process. You may have noticed I use the image of working out in the gym a lot in this book. I believe that the same principles taught in the gym work toward managing our struggle.

The Strengthening Process

1. Strengthen your resolve

You have to decide. No one can do this for you. How you think is how you will act. The power of this book is that I am attacking your mind. I am affronting your thoughts. Truth assaults a lie.

We struggle with making a decision because we are so afraid we will fail. After all, have we not been failing all along? What will change? How will this be different? That wall is too high. That goal is out of reach.

MAKE YOUR DECISION A DECLARATION.

Making the decision is the start. But you will still feel weak. Powerless. When you strengthen your resolve, you reinforce your decision with determination. Resolve infuses energy into your statement. This is why we see motivational coaches have their clients stand up, stand tall and shout their affirmation as loud as they can. They have them declare it before people. What does this do? It puts energy and force into the truth they are proclaiming. Emotion creates motion.

> When you strengthen your resolve, you reinforce your decision with determination.

To strengthen your resolve, you must fill yourself with motivation. This is the ever-critical WHY question you must answer...for yourself. Discovering your WHY energizes you. It builds resolve into your decision.

Ever seen a boxing movie? Rocky is the most famous. But there are a few others I have enjoyed watching as well. These are some of my favorite movies. Not because I like boxing. I like battle. Remember? I like blood and guts. Guts and glory.

Whenever the boxer gets knocked down, the referee starts to count him out. "1...2....3...4..." With the boxer sprawled about on the mat, the movie begins replaying scenes from the movie showing the boxer's family. They show him with his wife. With his child. They show him training with his coach cheering him on. They show him when he was struggling, with nothing. Seeing these images motivates the boxer to get up and keep fighting. He is not just fighting to win a boxing match, he is now fighting for his life.

"7...8..." The coach standing outside the ring is shouting "get up! GET UP!!" The crowd is cheering. The opponent boxer is already starting to celebrate that he has won. "....9!" Cue music. The boxer opens his eyes, picks himself up off the mat, and bumps his gloves ready to fight.

The climax of the movie happens at the end when the boxer fights his opponent, having little energy left, but mustering all the passion and drive he can. He knocks out the opponent and wins the battle. ....and the crowd goes wild!

Yo Adrienne...I DID IT!!

I cry every time I watch that scene. My wife will walk by me and give me a look of disgust, as if to say "really??!" I can't help it. Movies like that motivate me. They fire me up.

What fires you up? You need some motivation to strengthen your resolve. You need to stand up, stand tall and shout loud your decision. You need to make your decision a *declaration*. Feed your fire with fuel. For you, it may be something else. Find your fuel. And pour it on your goals like gas on a fire. Be resolved that you are going to press through, even when you get knocked down, even when you struggle with your struggle.

Listen to my favorite boxing hero, Rocky:

"Let me tell you something you already know. The world ain't all sunshine and rainbows. It's a very mean and nasty place, and I don't care how tough you are, it will beat you to your knees and keep you there permanently if you let it. You, me, or nobody is gonna hit as hard as life. But it ain't about how hard you hit. It's about how hard you can get hit and keep moving forward; how much you can take and keep moving forward. That's how winning is done! Now, if you know what you're worth, then go out and get what you're worth. But you gotta be willing to take the hits, and not pointing fingers saying you ain't where you wanna be because of him, or her, or anybody. Cowards do that and that ain't you. You're better than that! I'm always gonna love you, no matter what. No matter what happens. You're my son and you're my blood. You're the best thing in my life. But until you start believing in yourself, you ain't gonna have a life."

–Sylvester Stallone, Rocky Balboa

2. Strengthen your mindset

Just like you need motivation to strengthen your resolve, you need something to empower your mindset. You need the right mindset. You need a positive mindset.

I almost could call this section the power of positive thinking. Thinking positive has such power, yet most people do not realize how powerful it is for your mindset. I am a naturally positive person. I am a hopeless optimist, a high belief guy. I am always excited about the future. So, when I am with people who are realistic and skeptical, it rubs me wrong. I know that we have to face reality. But... how boring! How depressing. How about this? What if we could *change reality*? What if we could bring about positive change?

What if

A positive mindset believes we can change our circumstance which will lead to a brighter future. I love a *what if* person. A *what if* person looks at a problem and asks the question *what if*. When we use this approach with a positive attitude, it opens up fresh ideas and expands our possibilities.

What if I got 3 friends together and we started running together early in the morning once a week? How fun would that be? What would that do for my health? How much better would I sleep?

What if I could pay off this small credit card that I owe $350 on first? What would I have to sell to do that? Is there a side job I could take to raise additional money? Then, I could use that additional money to pay off the next big debt I owe!

What if I found my 5 favorite inspiring quotes, printed them on paper and taped them up on my bathroom mirror? Every morning, the first thing I would see is inspiration that would help motivate me. What would that do to reset my thinking and emotions as I started my day?

What if I asked two friends to ask me how I am doing with purity once a week? *What if* instead of finding a time to meet, we could simply text each other to make it easier with our schedules. Then, I would not be hiding my secret struggles, I would have invited accountability with support. That would help me not feel like I am all alone.

What if, instead of giving up all sugar and bread forever, I allowed myself a treat on Friday night for doing good all week? *What if* I used a treat as a reward for eating clean the rest of the week? *What if* my spouse and I agreed to do that together? Maybe I could find a healthier alternative for a nightly snack, because I know I am too weak to not have anything at night.

What now

You see, most of us fall into a *what now* mindset. A *what now* person always starts from a negative tone. A *what now* person is always waiting for the worst to happen.

> What happened now? I am always struggling, and I am always frustrated. So, **what now**?

> My friend has an idea for me to deal with my struggle. What does she want from me? **What now**?

> Nothing has happened good in my life. I hear change is coming at my work that will affect my job. This can't be good. **What now**?

A **what now** question positions you in a waiting posture. Let me coach you. Nothing good *ever comes* for those who just stand around waiting. All waiting does for you is make you worry. **What now** thinking looks for the bad and expects the worst. **What now** does not take any responsibility, no initiative to make things better. You are just waiting for something good to come to you. That is not how it works, friend. Why would God want to give a gift to someone who

All waiting does for you is make you worry

is standing around waiting with a sour look and a negative attitude? If you were a parent of a child like you, would you want to reward that kind of mindset?

A *what if* attitude will strengthen your mindset. **What if** questions activate your mind to greater possibilities? And they will fill your mind with energizing positivity. Negative thoughts pull you down. Positive thoughts lift you up. Use the power of positive thinking to strengthen your mindset muscles.

3. Strengthen your fences

A mentor told me how he keeps himself holy from sin and temptation. He used an analogy of a farm with animals. He said some animals are so strong and aggressive, that they can jump over the fences of the farm. For these animals, you have to build bigger fences so that they cannot escape. He told me that he has learned in some areas of weakness in his life, he has had to build taller fences that keep him from jumping over. The fences he has built have protected him from getting into dangerous areas that he knew he could not handle.

My friend was talking about the wisdom of setting up guardrails in his life. These guardrails keep him protected from walking outside a place of protection and safety where he can stay strong and remain faithful to God and to his family and friends.

> Like a city whose walls are broken through is a
> person who lacks self-control.
> Proverbs 25:28

Managing your struggle is not only about strengthening yourself, it is about strengthening your fences. It is about building some walls around areas of weakness. You must take personal responsibility for this. Don't walk through life exposed and unprotected. This goes hand in hand with setting a structure in your life with rules you will live by. The rules you set are your principles, while the walls you build are your protection. The reason you fail in abiding by

> The rules you set are your principles, while the walls you build are your protection.

your rules is that you are allowing temptations to attack you from all sides, at all times. When you build some high walls around your areas of weakness, you greatly reduce the amount of temptations that hit you. That's smart thinking. That's wisdom.

What walls can you construct? What fences do you need to mend? Let the walls do the work FOR YOU.

	Restrict access to internet, tv. Give codes to your spouse	
Never meet alone with a person of the opposite sex, or anyone who you have had inappropriate connection with.	**Your Struggle**	Do not have access to your bank accounts or any credit cards. You are given an allowance of cash for your needs and you have to show receipts for everything.
	Never travel alone. Always with a trusted colleague or friend. You have a GPS tracker on your cell phone that your spouse and friend can see where you are at all times.	

Ok. When you read these walls I listed, you are probably thinking "Dude! Get real. What is this? The Gestapo? What are you? My dad?"

Well, actually, yes. I am your dad. Yes. I am the police. You need a parent, remember? These rules may be too strict for you. But, in some form, I practice these in my own life. They look different at different seasons where I feel I am weak in some areas. But I set up my own fences of accountability. I do this, because I appreciate my life. God has given me a beautiful wife. Two awesome kids. He has given me great friends, a great church, and a great calling.

I love what I get to do. I see God working in me and through me. I would never want to disqualify myself from getting to do what He has gifted me to do. I would never want to dishonor my wife and family with bad decisions in a moment of weakness. So, I have put some restrictive walls up in areas of my life. These are just a few. I have more that guard me in other areas.

The walls I listed above have to do with purity, relationship, and financial management. If your struggle is with anxiety, what walls do you need to build around you? How about anger? What will those walls need to be? What about physical health, a struggle for all of us. What are the four walls that you will construct to protect you?

Before you throw this book out and start calling me a lunatic trying to take over your life, let me ask you a question: does the company you work at require that you live by restrictions? Does your supervisor require a weekly report showing where you went, what you spent, and what you produced? Mine does.

I have found an interesting pattern with people who own their own business: many of them are overwhelmed and out of balance in their life. Amazing! Why is that? I find that they have no one guiding them and speaking into their life. So what do they do? They reach out to me for help. I have business owners calling me all the time needing care and support because their marriage is struggling, or their health is failing, or their kids are not making good choices. They can't keep employees to stay in their company because they don't treat them well. What they desperately need is someone to help them build fences in areas of their life. Only then, they can experience a healthy, full life.

Have you ever talked with a UPS delivery driver? My brother is one. He tells me that UPS tracks their every move on a GPS device. They have recently installed cameras in the truck so they can watch their drivers throughout the day. UPS does not just track your packages, they track their drivers! If the driver is stalling or moving too slow, they get coached. If the driver ever pulls out his cell phone to answer a text, they get corrected...sternly. It's a warning before they are terminated. My brother says "I am aware that I am on their time. I am on their clock." Is this harsh? Maybe. But, UPS is paying for results. And they have studied that efficiency leads to effectiveness.

> High walls eliminate the distraction of temptation.

High walls and strong fences keep you moving efficiently so you can work effectively. Just like a racehorse wears blinders around his eyes, you need walls to block off distractions so you can focus forward.

God has given you so many great blessings in your life. Stop and look at what you have. You have people who love you. You have life. You have God-given gifts. God has designed you with a purpose and a destiny to fulfill. When you protect yourself with high walls and strong fences, you can eliminate the distraction of temptation. Building fences will help you focus on the purpose God has for you.

Strengthen the fences that have broken down. Build some high walls around your weakness, and respect the walls. I know you don't have a boss to tell you what to do. So then, be your own boss. Take leadership of your life and supervise yourself! Allow some others to help supervise you. You need it. It's good for you to answer for your actions. It's good to be accountable to trusted people. I answer to people. So should you.

4. Strengthen your body

Build your body. Am I talking about your physical body? Well, certainly. Yes. I believe physical fitness helps us to feel strong and think clear. There is so much to be learned by fitness and bodybuilding. I have leaned into this more than ever. Now, I look better, I feel better, I think better. I have discovered that when I begin to see results physically, I soon see results spiritually, relationally, financially, emotionally. Mind, Body, Spirit.

With that being said, I want to focus you on building your *spirit* as well. Earlier, I focused on your mind, strengthening your resolve and your mindset. Your physical body is connected to your mind and your spirit. And while you need to put the time investment in to caring for your body and building your body, building your spirit is the key to it all.

Finally, be strong in the Lord and in his mighty power. Put on the full armor of God, so that you can take your stand against the devil's schemes. For our struggle is not against flesh and blood, but against the rulers, against the authorities, against the powers of this dark world and against the spiritual forces of evil in the heavenly realms. Therefore put on the full armor of God, so that when the day of evil comes, you may be able to stand your ground, and after you have done everything, to stand. Stand firm then, with the belt of truth buckled around your waist, with the breastplate of righteousness in place, and with your feet fitted with the readiness that comes from the gospel of peace. In addition to all this, take up the shield of

faith, with which you can extinguish all the flaming arrows of the evil one. Take the helmet of salvation and the sword of the Spirit, which is the word of God.
And pray in the Spirit on all occasions with all kinds of prayers and requests. With this in mind, be alert and always keep on praying for all the Lord's people.
Ephesians 6:10-18

I love this verse! This is that guts-and-glory battle cry I am so drawn to. The Apostle Paul vividly captures the struggle that we all face when we choose to follow Jesus Christ as the leader of our lives. This is why I love Paul. He is a leader I can follow. He is a man with a struggle, a thorn in his flesh that he must learn to master and work to manage. Paul loved Jesus. Paul desired to live holy before God. But he struggled. He was in a battle. And that battle was spiritual, though it manifests in the physical.

Spiritual Battle

If you are not familiar with this scripture, we Christians quote this often, declaring to one another "put on the full armor of God." To build your body, you must build your spirit. Your physical body lives only for a few years. But your spirit lives on forever. (James 4:13-17) Just like you have to build your body and build your mindset, you have to build your spirit.

Be strong in the Lord and in His mighty power

Put on the full armor of God

Pray in the Spirit

These references all have to do with being built up, being prepared and battling – in your spirit. And we build *our* spirit through *God's* Spirit. That is the Holy Spirit. In ourselves, we can do nothing. Our spirit cannot be strong unless we are connected to God. (John 15.) We must literally have the Holy Spirit living *in us*. (1 Corinthians 3:16, 2 Timothy 1:14, Ephesians 5:18, Romans 8:11)

Putting on the full armor of God is how we build our spirit. This is why reading God's Word and memorizing it are two powerful practices. Ephesians gives us a powerful three-step punch to fend off the attack of Satan:

1. Be Strong

2. Put On

3. Pray In

How Your Enemy Attacks

The enemy of our soul is working overtime to attack you. While you are having to grapple with your struggle, Satan tries to use it to defeat you. His attacks of lies, discouragement, fear, excuses, and compromise are all meant to keep you anemic and feeling weak. When you listen to and accept his attacks, Satan's mission is accomplished.

The enemy will mock the armor of God. He will minimize the importance of reading God's Word. He will dismiss praying and fasting as useless. He will make fun of submitting yourself and restricting yourself. The enemy's temptation is *to do what thou wilt*. The enemy will always question God's Word by asking *did God really say that?*

"For our struggle is not with flesh and blood..." reveals that our struggle is not really physical, but spiritual. We must understand that our enemy is not difficult people or difficult circumstances. Only when we know who are enemy is and how they attack will we then understand the importance of preparing for the battle. That is done by building our spirit.

When we take the time to strengthen our spirit, management becomes a lot easier. You might think that strengthening only happens in the mastering phase. It does. Certainly. You were weak. Now, you have built muscles to be able to overcome your struggle. But strengthening is an ongoing practice. It must be a new normal in our routine. To stay strong you must always get strong.

Conclusion

As we strengthen our resolve, strengthen our mindset, strengthen our fences and strengthen our spirit, we will stay strong to manage our struggles. Management simply becomes a daily system we live by. Management is work to be sure. But the work will become manageable.

This next chapter will tackle some trouble areas we all deal with. Keeping to the theme of this book, I want to show you how can you turn a negative into a positive. You can use what works against you *for* you. God chooses to leave your struggle in your life to shape your life. We get to choose how it will shape us, either for the better or for the worse. This next section will be helpful to you.

Chapter 7

The Helpful Seven

Great character, like massive roots grow deep when water is
sparse and winds are strong.
–Charles Swindoll

I want this book to be really practical. Inspiring? Yes.
Motivational? You better believe it. But I want to do more
than just make you feel better. I want you to *get* better.
Build bigger. To build bigger, you have to go deeper. *Grow*
deeper.

Thus far, I have shown you how to be aware of your struggle
and how to view it. I have given you the tools on to master
your struggle, and then manage it. In this chapter, I want
to address some of life's challenges that you will face. When
you are doing the hard work of overcoming your struggle,
one would think that others would cheer you on. Being in a
stress-free, controlled environment of encouragement and
support would certainly be optimal as you climb uphill.

Yet, life is not so easy. People are not as sensitive to your
needs as you would like. As Rocky Balboa said, *"the world
ain't full of sunshine and rainbows."* To press through the
pressures of life, you are going to have to put your big boy
pants on.

I call these areas the Helpful Seven. Seven areas for Chapter 7. Wait a second...how could the pressures of life be helpful? How could my hurts help me? I can't see how frustration could be my friend.

You need to learn to use everything that comes against you to help you grow. These areas have a tendency to keep us stuck and get us off focus. To grow, you must move forward. How you see your struggle determines your future success. Likewise, these helpful seven can actually build your life and character. God allows everything in your life for a reason. Your job is to find out why it is there.

1. Fear

Fear is paralyzing. Nothing will stop you dead in your tracks like being scared. But many times, we are scared of a ghost. That fear is usually a fake. There is no real flesh and bones to what we concoct in our heads. And if something bad happens that we fear, it is not as bad as we thought.

Believe it or not, fear can actually help us. It can help us grow in that every time we move forward in the face of fear, we destroy it's power over us. We prove it false. Standing strong in the face of one fear will build our confidence to stand in the face of the next one. Courage is not the absence of fear, it is standing in the midst of it.

We demolish arguments and every pretension
that sets itself up against the knowledge of
God, and we take captive every thought to make
it obedient to Christ.
2 Corinthians 10:15

The next time you face fear, whether it is real or not, make the decision to put your faith before your fear. If you have surrendered your life to the Lordship of Christ, your faith is not just in your own power and wisdom. Your faith is in God. Put your faith in His promises that are true. Your fears will be turned to fiction as your faith grows.

2. Discomfort

Doing new things can be exciting for some. But for most, new can translate to uncomfortable. Likely, all of the new thinking and habits you will begin practicing will be uncomfortable. I mean, to overcome a struggle, you know that means you are going to have to embrace habits that are different and difficult.

> Put your faith before your fear.

They certainly won't be eating more ice cream at night and charging on credit cards on a whim. No. The habits that will get you where you want to be will feel restrictive.

We already addressed the power of pain and the success that comes from structure. And while those will certainly hurt, I want to prepare you for the feeling of being in uncomfortable settings. You are going to be in new environments with new people. You are being thrust into a faster pace with higher expectations. Your journey is uphill and there is no rest stop to grab a slurpy. Prepare yourself for uncomfortable feelings in unfamiliar territory.

> GET COMFORTABLE WITH BEING UNCOMFORTABLE

This is a new normal you are going to have to get comfortable with. Every time you feel uncomfortable, take a breath and tell yourself to keep moving forward, one step at a time. Every time you feel out of place, stay humble and stay engaged.

Feeling uncomfortable can be triggered in many ways. Here are some that I have had to push through:

> I am brand new to a team of people who have been part of the team for a long time. I feel like I don't belong. I want to go back to where I am known.

> I am just starting out in learning a skill, while others have mastered the skill and are running circles around me. I feel foolish, and want to go back to where I am skilled.

> I messed up and was corrected by my supervisor. I hate feeling like I am in trouble or that I failed. I just want to go where I can win easily.

> I feel restricted by someone else's rules and style preference. I feel inhibited and want my own freedom to do what I want, how I want, when I want.

> I am not the leader in the group and therefore am not taken seriously when I have ideas or opinions. I want to be heard, so I want to go back to friends who see me as the leader.

> My gifts are not being fully used and I do not feel appreciated. I am doing the work while someone else is getting the credit. I want to go back to the place where I can shine.

OK. I just let you in on some of my inner struggles. These are areas that I have had to submit to God and submit to leaders to stay in a healthy place. Can you relate to any of these? Did I hit a nerve? These feelings are uncomfortable. Remember that pain will move us.

If the pain is a result of your bad decisions, then let it push you to healthy life change. But if the pain is because of feeling uncomfortable with moving in a healthy life direction, then stay the course. Suck it up! Push through. Go back to strengthening your resolve! Be tough. Don't be easy on yourself. Refrain from blame. Keep going.

3. Adversity

I like to watch a lot of online coaches teach how to lose fat and build muscle. Because they are creating a media presentation, the video will have catchy music, great lighting, and a well-designed set. The speaker coaching in the video is jacked with muscles and 5 percent body fat.

They share the seven steps to lose fat and build muscle. What they don't speak much of, or what they tend to minimize is the adversity that will come in the process. If you were naïve, you would finish the video thinking "this is actually pretty easy. I can do this!" That's what I feel after every video. However, I am slapped with the reality that it is not as easy to get that six pack of abs.

You already know what a struggle feels like and looks like. I want to remind you that you will have adversity along your journey. *Duh.*

Strength does not come from winning. Your struggles develop your strengths. When you go through hardships and decide not to surrender, that is strength.
–Mahatma Gandhi

Adversity will help you remember your WHY and will refine your focus. Adversity is a great teacher. You can use it to toughen you up. But you will also discover the realities of what is achievable and what is not worth trying to achieve. Adversity can become a reality check.

I used to think I could get down to 190 lbs, and maybe lower. However, with balancing other parts of my life, and realizing what diet and exercise regimen I would have to adhere to in order to achieve that, I eventually adjusted my goal to 200 lbs. I am close right now, being at 206. I reached a weight last year below 200 lbs for a few months, but life happened and I grew to 210. With management, I have reached 206 lbs and have maintained. Soon, I am going to make a decision to focus myself in a season of the year when I can give myself space to fully commit to a calorie cut to reach my goal of 200 lbs. What helped me arrive at this softer goal was the adversity that I faced with a busy career, traveling and life responsibilities.

Adversity has certainly helped me remember my WHY to keep pushing through. But it has also been a tool to refine what I focus on, and when. I have become more adaptable and calculated. Timing and attention to all aspects of my life play into my goals.

You cannot stay rigid through adversity. You must learn to navigate through it in order to keep moving forward in a positive way. Use adversity to toughen your resolve and remember your WHY. But also use adversity to mature you and make you more measured and thoughtful.

4. Criticism

I hate criticism. There. I admit it. I have discovered that I am a sensitive person. OK. I will admit that I am insecure at times. Well, all the time. Don't criticize my insecurity!

Few people love criticism. Most people do not take criticism well. This is likely because we all have a measure of sensitivity and insecurity if we are honest. A word of criticism or correction cuts to our pride as if to demean our very identity.

Studies have shown that people are not open to criticism unless outnumbered by praises. The Gottman Institute shares that the secret to a happy marriage is to pour on praise and kindness when dealing with a negative conflict or conversation:

Their discovery was simple. The difference between happy and unhappy couples is the balance between positive and negative interactions during conflict. There is a very specific ratio that makes love last. That "magic ratio" is 5 to 1. This means that for every negative interaction during conflict, a stable and happy marriage has five (or more) positive interactions.
–Kyle Bensen published October 4, 2017,
The Gottman Institute, Gottman.com

5 to 1. Wouldn't that be nice? When your spouse is frustrated because you didn't remember their birthday, they first give you five positive affirmations? How about when your boss has to correct you on a mishandled project but starts by giving you five reasons she appreciates you? Hardly.

Criticism rarely comes with sunshine and rainbows. Correction does not wait until we are good and ready. People will tell you what they think when they think it. Most people speak first, then consider their words and tone later.

It's hard enough to hear criticism from someone who you know loves you, like your spouse. It's hard enough to take correction from someone who believes in you and hired you, like your boss. What is wounding is to receive criticism from people who don't care about you or who don't really know you.

My mom has helped me navigate how to handle criticism and correction. She was a school teacher and a pastor's wife. She was in positions that always garnered other people's opinions and expectations. My mom coached me with great insight:

> Matt, you can use criticism as a tool to improve yourself. Even if people mean it for harm, you can use it for good. Find the nugget of truth, and leave the rest.

My mom had a high belief in herself. She paid her own way through college. She raised three children. She continued her education by building a successful career where she impacted hundreds of students. She started me with piano lessons and drove me to my teacher every week for many years, sacrificing her money and her time. She helped my dad start a church and helped lead and build the church. My mom has led many into a relationship with Jesus Christ. Yet, my mom had her own hurts and struggles that she had to battle through.

I saw her navigate through seasons of great pain and personal disappointments. I saw her at times overwhelmed with the weight of having too much to carry, from home, to church to career. Yet, she pressed forward, trusting in God, with a vibrant prayer life and a daily habit of reading God's Word. My mom is one of my heroes. She is tough on the inside and sweet on the outside. She has great wisdom to teach, based on real-world experience. I have lived by her advice of using criticism to help me improve my life.

I have used criticism both from people who love me, and from those who do not believe in me.

People who are more mature can process criticism and correction faster than those who are immature. A person with greater emotional capacity can stay grounded in their identity and in their calling. They have the emotional capacity to keep moving forward, while people with small emotional capacity take criticism personally, letting it wound them deeply.

> **People who are more mature can process criticism and correction faster than those who are immature.**

It takes small people several days and even weeks to talk about the criticism and be bothered by it before they are themselves again. Big people (emotionally) also get wounded by criticism. They deal with it in a healthy way.

Emotionally healthy people have learned to rest well after the criticism comes. They don't react right away. They respond by resting. Once they have rested (more on rest in a later chapter), they go to God through prayer and reading His Word. It is in prayer and in reading God's Word that reminds us of Who God is and who we are in Christ. From this place, they can now begin to reflect on the criticism, dissecting what is helpful from what is hurtful. They find the truth in the criticism and then apply it to their life in a way that they can begin constructing a plan to improve. Once a plan is formed, they start learning, practicing and improving.

Big people always remain humble through this process. Yet, big people are hopeful they will grow and become stronger and better for greater impact. Through this process, they stay focused on what God has called them to do. They use criticism to propel them forward into their assignment.

Healthy Process for Handling Criticism/Correction

1. **Respond** by resting

2. **Remind** yourself who God is and who you are in Christ

4. **Reflect** to find the truth that is helpful

5. **Rehearse** your growth process to improve

5. Offense

How easily are you offended? What does it take to get you out of whack? What are your triggers?

It amazes me how angry drivers get when another driver cuts them off on the road. You would have thought the person cutting them off killed their mother. Yet people can be thrown into a rampage just by having to wait in line or having to slow down on the road because another driver unintentionally moved ahead of them. And, even if the driver was reckless or being mean, why would one let that create rage in them?

Our country is divided politically, creating a perfect scenario for a brush fire to catch wind. Major altercations can happen when someone speaks of their favorite political hero or party. People feel the need to attack a political personality they have never met, and defend a political party they do not fully understand.

Make sure to steer clear of offense. Settle down. Focus in. It is going to take all of your energy and heart to overcome your struggle. Don't waste time with frivolous arguments and debates. Your emotions can be powerful in your life. They can be used to energize your goals or energize your destructive habits. Positive emotions are needed to climb uphill. Negative emotions will pull you downhill.

John Bevere wrote a great book, *The Bait of Satan* that deals with being offended. The title speaks for itself. He shows us how our enemy uses an offense to knock us off our mission.

> "Bitterness is a root. If roots are nursed—watered, protected, fed, and given attention—they increase in depth and strength. If not dealt with quickly, roots are hard to pull up. The strength of the offense will continue to grow. We are therefore exhorted not to let the sun go down on our wrath. (See Ephesians 4:26.) Now instead of the fruit of righteousness being produced, we will see a harvest of anger, resentment, jealousy, hatred, strife, and discord. Jesus called these evil fruits."
> —John Bevere, Bait Of Satan: Living Free from the Deadly Trap of Offense

We want to produce the fruit of righteousness, that is doing what God has called us to do. Love God and love people. When I think of fruit mentioned in the Bible, my mind immediately goes to the fruit of the Spirit.

But the fruit of the Spirit is love, joy, peace, forbearance, kindness, goodness, faithfulness, gentleness and self-control. Against such things there is no law.
Galatians 5:22-23 NIV

Life is not about you.	This is what righteousness looks like. This is how it tastes. Sweet like the ripest berry you ever ate. Nothing in this description tastes offensive. In

fact, offense is the exact opposite of love, joy, peace, forbearance, kindness, goodness, faithfulness, gentleness and self-control. Oh, that we would be more like these fruits!

How can we use an offense to help us? Grow your emotional maturity by realizing the offense is powerless to hurt you. *You* have the power to allow something to offend you or not. If someone cuts you off on the road, let it go. Be forbearing. Let them go first. If someone gets angry with you for talking politics, make peace. Have a gentle spirit. Live in joy. Look for ways to be kind to people who are different than you. When someone does offend you, use self-control and stay faithful to what God has called you to focus on. Love, even when you don't receive it.

When you realize that not everyone is going to like you or agree with you, you can love them and move on. Offense is a trap. The bait of Satan. Don't be so easily lured. See offense for what it is, a petty trick of the enemy to slow you down and move you off course to be on mission for God's purpose for your life.

6. Comparison

Nothing will steal your joy more quickly than comparison. The Bible actually lists comparison in the Big 10: The Ten Commandments. "Do not covet your neighbor's _____." (Exodus 20:17) Fill in the blank. Whatever your neighbor has, stop wishing you had it.

Life is not a competition. Life is meant to be enjoyed. Now, you may be a person who loves competition. I know.

I understand. I love competition. I love to win. Not at everything, but at least what I feel I am good at.

I, I, I, I. A lot of I's there. That's the root of the problem with comparison. We are so concerned with outdoing our friends or outshining our competitors, that we miss the blessings God has given us. We miss the great because we somehow believe we can have greater. This becomes unhealthy really fast, thinking that there is something we are missing, or something that is better. We miss the joy of seeing what God has in store for us. Consequently, we alienate good friends and family, because no one wants to be around a frustrated, self-centered person.

Here's a hard truth I want to confront you with: life is not about you. Your purpose, your gifts, and your blessings are not for you. They are to help others. You are to serve people. Not impress people – serve people. That means if you don't get to use your gift the way you dream about, then so be it.

God has given you so much. And yes, He wants to bless your life. But He wants to bless *through* your life. If your goal is the be the greatest so that people praise you, you have missed the purpose of your blessing. You will always be wanting more, never feeling content. That is an empty feeling, a dark place to be.

Learn to trust God with your life and your season. Appreciate what He has given you, and accept what He has not. Certainly, you can have ambition and desire. God gave you that to achieve greatness. But on your own, you are incomplete. No human achievement or worldly success can make you complete. Only a relationship with God can.

Here is how the temptation of comparison can be helpful in overcoming your struggle. When you see someone else who seems to be in a better position than you, use it as encouragement for yourself. When someone else is farther along in reaching their dreams, celebrate with them. *Positive emotion creates forward motion.* When you celebrate others, you attract them to you. You need positive people celebrating you. So, give to others what you would appreciate from them.

A grateful spirit attracts the generosity of God and others. Don't hate others. Help them. You will find that celebrating frees you from the need to compare. No need to keep track of your competition. Rather, use your energy to propel you forward, not pull others down.

7. Apathy

Apathy is interesting. It is subtle, yet complex. Apathy is likely the most difficult to identify in ourselves, because it lays on the ground floor in our emotions and mindset. There could be a few reasons why we will grapple with this subtle setback:

TIRED

I find that apathy creeps in to my mindset when I realize how tired I am. I am a driver. I have passion and purpose bursting within me, like a steam roller train chugging along. However, when I become depleted, I can have feelings of no motivation. My mind becomes foggy, my pace slow, my attitude, uncaring. I hate this feeling, because I feel like there is more to accomplish, more I am called to do.

Here is how I use apathy to help me get back on track. I use it as a meter to read my vital signs. We are not good self-regulators. The reason why we catch a cold or gain unwanted weight is that we tend to move too fast and not rest. We think that we can go harder, work longer, and accomplish more. But our bodies, our emotions and our spirit are all delicate. We have limits. Like a vehicle, we need to be maintained. Oil needs changing. Tires need rotation. Spark plugs need replacing.

I am going to dedicate an entire chapter to regulation and rest. But in this section, I wanted to connect how apathy can be used to be helpful.

FAMILIAR

Apathy can also set in when we live in the familiar too long. While consistency and steadiness create a conducive environment for overcoming struggles, we need a challenge. If we aren't challenged, what once felt fun and familiar becomes boring and tedious. Feelings of apathy can weigh us down, keeping us from feeling fresh and agile so we can charge forward with our focused goals.

Depending on your personality, this will look different for you. This all goes back to self-regulating yourself. *You* know *you*. *You* know what *you* can handle. Or do you?

While we want to monitor our emotions and watch our limits, we also need to test our limits. This takes stretching ourselves and testing our boundaries..

One of my friends, Brandon, is a Pastor I get to work with. He and I recently took on some additional responsibilities within our church, areas that had never previously been defined. Brandon and I are learning how to be effective as leaders, wanting to help people to drive our church's mission forward in a positive way. We meet together with a team to discuss how we can lead effectively, having never done this before.

I heard Brandon share some ideas that he was implementing in his areas of responsibility. I was shocked that he was so bold and risky to step out and try new ideas. I asked "do you have permission to do that?" Brandon said "I don't know." I questioned "Brandon, how do you know if you have crossed a boundary?" Brandon, smiling back at me, and responded with "I will know when I cross one."

Being around friends like Brandon sharpens me and keeps me thinking fresh. Because I am in a space of more responsibility, with more expectation of positive results, I am far from apathetic. I have been a Pastor for many years. But church ministry is changing rapidly, and I am being forced to learn new concepts and paradigms of today's culture. What I am learning is that every task I do and every investment of time and money I make counts big. I do not have a lot of margin for error. I cannot afford to be lazy in decisions or sloppy in execution.

This is scary *and* exciting all at the same time for me. I am a student, an amateur who is learning every day. I am taking calculated risks and observing people who are more experienced and more skilled – and I am learning from them. New habits. New experiments. Study, correct, and try again.

Observe ➡ Test ➡ Try ➡ Study ➡ Correct ➡ Try Again

Let's look at some areas in your life where you need to be stretched out of the familiar:

CAREER

What season are you in at work? Are you doing the same events and tasks every year? Do you go to the same restaurant with the same co-workers every week? What new project are you contributing to that is out of your familiar? What co-workers are you building rapport with that are different than you? What new circles of influence are you building?

MARRIAGE

How about your marriage? Is it flat? Are you more like partners than lovers? What is a new hobby you have tried with your spouse? What fun trip are you planning together to create a new experience?

HEALTH

What about your workout routine? Tired of doing 30 minutes on the treadmill listening to the same podcast? Is your workout honestly too easy to do? Same spin class with friends who are just there to chat? Are you ready to hit the weights and push yourself in a more intense workout? What about asking some Crossfit superstars if you could join their workout for a day?

SKILL

How have you improved? Can you measure it? Are you relying too heavily on your gifts to get by? How about identifying a skill that would help you have more impact. Study it. Work on it. Practice it.

In some area of your life, it may be time to change it up. Put some spice in your life. If you are not sure how to do this, take a free morning when you are feeling fresh and chart out on a white board an area of your life. Treat it like a business or a project at work. Work on yourself. Be your own coach, and coach yourself up! You probably need a stretch. You may be ready for a challenge.

Use apathy as a challenge meter. If your passion is low, so is your challenge. If your motivation is tight, it may mean that your muscles need a stretch. Rather than let apathy keep you low and tight, let it be an indicator that you need a coach to challenge you. A challenge will stretch you, pushing you to test your boundaries. Don't be afraid if you stretch too far. You will know when you reach your limit – it is when you cross your boundaries. Testing will exhilarate your spirit and catapult you beyond your familiar. It will allow you to reach another level of victory over your struggle.

Conclusion

To build bigger, your roots have to go deeper. Charles Swindoll shows us the growth process of a tree, pointing to growth through sparse water and heavy winds. That's why I call these areas my

Helpful Seven:

1. Fear

2. Discomfort

3. Adversity

4. Criticism

5. Offense

6. Comparison

7. Apathy

Part of self-leadership is learning to be self-aware. When there are pressures and pains happening around you, stop and ask what is going on *inside* of you?" This list of my *Helpful Seven* may not feel like they are very helpful. But you can learn to turn a negative in to a positive. You can use these hurts as helpful toward deepening your roots. Remember that roots are not seen. They are hidden. In order to see the growth of the tree and fruit growing from the branches, the root system has to be bigger. To sustain the tree, the roots have to become stronger.

You need to grow bigger in your thinking. Bigger in your character. Bigger in your emotional capacity. Stronger in your systems and in your healthy habits. The *Helpful Seven* will train you well. When Rocky was training for his upcoming boxing match, Rocky's crotchety, old boxing coach, Micky shouted at Rocky during his training: "get up! Micky loves you!" You too need some tough training and some tough love. You are preparing for battle! You are training for your match! (can you hear the Rocky theme music playing? I can...)

Now, with all of this tough battle talk, you will need a secret ingredient that will help you withstand the *Helpful Seven*. Being tough can only last so long before you wear out. You are human. You get tired. In fact, it is your humanness and weakness that directly attributes to your struggle. In order for you to make it through all of the tough steps you have to take in order to overcome your struggle, check out this powerful, secret ingredient. This will help you like nothing else can. This will infuse your life with tons of energy and passion that you need to press on. It will make you stronger so you can continue to strengthen!

Chapter 8

The Secret Ingredient

MUSCLES ARE TORN IN THE GYM
FED IN THE KITCHEN
BUILT IN THE BED

The title of this chapter probably has you guessing "what is the secret ingredient?" Hopefully, I have created suspense for you, to pull you in. My quote above may have already given you a clue... or maybe it is still unclear. That's alright. The ingredient I speak of is, indeed a secret. Most people struggle with this secret I am thinking of. Most would not think of this as important. I sure didn't realize how essential this secret ingredient is to strengthening, at least until just a few years ago.

... before I reveal just exactly what this secret ingredient is.... (more suspense, cliff hanger)

I want you to know that I researched as I wrote this book. I am a student who is thirsty to learn and understand. Some of my research comes from my own experiences growing up. One of my childhood heroes is a martial artist and movie star, Bruce Lee. Most boys growing up in my generation watched martial arts movies, standing in front of the tv imitating the moves, the kicks and the sounds. "haiiiyyyahh!"

Bruce Lee was arguably the best martial artist who has ever lived. What made him the best was not his size or his strength. It was his mindset to be a lifelong learner. His drive for personal improvement made in him a master martial artist. At a very young age, he was already a teacher to many students, as he owned his own training center. Even Hollywood stars sought out Bruce Lee, becoming his student.

I can relate with Bruce Lee's learner-mindset. I also esteem to continually grow and develop myself. This quote from Bruce Lee resonates with who I am:

"Ever since I was a child I have had this instinctive urge for expansion and growth. To me, the function and duty of a quality human being is the sincere and honest development of one's potential."
–Bruce Lee

We all desire to expand. At least, we should. We should expand our strength and our health. We should expand our relationships. We should expand our knowledge. We should expand our impact and our influence in the world. Bruce Lee expanded himself, which expanded his reach to people. His life made a positive impact in the world.

The sad part of Bruce Lee's life was that it ended in tragedy. He died of a Cerebral Edema, a swelling in the brain that was caused by an allergic reaction from pain medication. Bruce Lee was a healthy, 32 year old man. He ate healthy and was in perfect physical shape, having sculpted his body with intensive exercise. Bruce Lee was a very disciplined individual. You don't get to be a master martial artist without great work and discipline. Bruce was also a hard worker, making movies, tv shows, teaching martial arts, managing business opportunities, all while being a husband and father. He had a great life. He was on top of the world, making his Epic film, Enter the Dragon. Yet with all of his success, his untimely death was all that more tragic. It is reported that 25,000 people attended his funeral held in Hong Kong. His loyal fans showed their sadness and disbelief that their young hero had died too soon.

Bruce Lee's death created much speculation. Some conspiracy theorists had suggested a dark, sinister plan by his enemies to kill him. Some have said that there was a curse on Bruce Lee's family, brought about because he revealed ancient Chinese secrets to the world. His son, Brandon Lee was later killed at an early age while shooting film for a Hollywood movie. This reinforced the curse theory. The speculation around Bruce Lee spurred curiosity by avid fans, much because it is difficult to understand why a young, healthy man would die at such a young age at the top of his game.

Want to know my theory? What do I think is the reason Bruce Lee died so unexpectedly? I am no doctor. I have no empirical evidence to show you what happened in his body. Bruce Lee died back in the seventies. I was just a child then. I wasn't there, so can't say for sure. But here is what I think attributed to Bruce's death: he was pushing too hard. He was always working. He had too much going on, working seven days a week. He admittedly pushed his body to the very limits to test his abilities. He would literally experiment with machines to see how much power he could get out of his muscles.

My theory is that Bruce Lee simply *wore himself out*. Plain and simple.

So, still want to know what I think is the secret ingredient to strengthening?

Rest

> # MUSCLES ARE TORN IN THE GYM
> # FED IN THE KITCHEN
> # BUILT IN THE BED

When I started getting passionate about my physical health, I realized that the secret to burning fat was building muscle. So, I started learning how to use weights to do what is called resistance exercise. As I continued learning the process of building muscle, I learned another important aspect of building muscle. *I discovered the secret ingredient to building muscle was rest.* Experts in muscle building stress the importance of resting your muscles immediately after you work your muscles. That quote above suggests that muscles are *built in the bed*, meaning when you rest and sleep, your muscles can repair and get stronger.

The process of muscle building is that when you lift heavy weights, your muscles actually tear. When you stretch your muscles, your muscles expand, allowing flexibility before you begin to tear them. Wow – that all sounds pretty drastic, doesn't it? Tearing? Well, it is. You are actually breaking down your muscle tissue, which is why resting them immediately after your workout allows them to repair. When you allow your body to rest properly, you actually build bigger muscles and create a stronger body. Then, the next time you work out your muscles, you break them down so you can build them even bigger!

Another term I hear trainers use is *fail*. They coach their audience to do the muscle-building exercises until fail. What? Like, until you can't do the exercise anymore? Yes. The only way you are going to make muscle gains is if you push your body to lift until you cannot hardly move. Then, you are to ingest some type of protein before you rest. Some say you should rest from exercise at least a day. Many say as much as two to three days! No exercise! At least not in the area of muscle that you just let "fail."

This was such a remarkable concept for me. Push your muscles until fail, and then don't exercise for a couple of days. I love this. I used to feel guilty because I was only going to the gym twice a week and for only about 20 minutes (I get bored after about 20 minutes of hard work in the gym.) Actually, the experts were telling me that this rhythm was the BEST strategy for muscle gain. Exercise done using proper technique and high intensity would produce the body strength and sculpting that we all desire.

OK. Let's apply this muscle-building principle to our process in how we learn to overcome our struggle.

What you need is rest. Desperately. Your life depends on it. While I do not know exactly why Bruce Lee died, I have a sneaking suspicion that he did not rest well. He did not know how to slow down, stop and rest. All he did was push, improve, work, travel, teach, produce. But he did not have good health (although his body was a work of art.) He suffered from headaches and fatigue. His life had a big impact, but it was cut short. Bruce Lee was a man of great vision and drive. What more could he have produced and enjoyed if he had lived to 60, 70, 80, 90? What would have happened if he would have built in a regimen of rest in his life?

The Bible has a word that describes rest. In fact, the word that God uses for rest is a command He gives us:

Sabbath

Sabbath means rest. However, Sabbath has deeper meaning. If you know anything about church or the Bible, you know Sabbath is actually a day of the week. Sabbath for most Christians falls on Sunday. However, the Bible identifies Saturday as the Sabbath on the Jewish calendar. Jews who abide by the Law of Moses observe the Sabbath carefully. Business owners close their businesses. No one is allowed to labor for 24 hours. Families actually prepare the food they will eat the day before the Sabbath, so they do not labor. The day is meant for family time, for worship of God and for rest from work.

Below is an excerpt from the Ten Commandments in the Bible. This commandment comes directly from God speaking to His holy people, Israel:

Observe the Sabbath day, to keep it holy, as the Lord your God commanded you. Six days you shall labor and do all your work, but the seventh day **is** the Sabbath of the Lord your God. **In it** you shall do no work: you, nor your son, nor your daughter, nor your male servant, nor your female servant, nor your ox, nor your donkey, nor any of your cattle, nor your stranger who **is** within your gates, that your male servant and your female servant may rest as well as you. And remember that you were a slave in the land of Egypt, and the Lord your God brought you out from there by a mighty hand and by an outstretched arm; therefore the Lord your God commanded you to keep the Sabbath day.
Deuteronomy 5:14 NKJV

Author, Lance Witt emphasizes the importance of the Sabbath day by saying "Sabbath is a commandment, not just a suggestion." Most of us understand the importance of work ethic. Your parents, teachers or coaches instilled in you principles of discipline and mental toughness. However, the importance of Sabbath likely was not taught with the same consistency. You understand that to get ahead you have to do more. To reach success, you have to be willing to work extra hours and push hard. How many times have you heard a motivational speaker or coach preach about getting up at 4 AM in the morning to go to the gym? How many times have you heard entrepreneurs brag about their stories of working all day and all night to do what was necessary to get their business off the ground?

We live in a world that celebrates success. We are conditioned to seek fame and finances. While success is good to aim for, the question is, at what cost?

I am not saying you have to forgo success for Sabbath. On the contrary. I am saying that practicing Sabbath will propel your success! Big time.

Sabbath is God's secret ingredient that He gives you.... actually....that He GIFTS YOU...to help you be successful, and stay successful throughout your full life. Yet, because God's ways are higher than our ways, and God's thoughts are not our thoughts, we will struggle to understand how stopping, resting and working less actually help us accomplish more. So, God does not just suggest Sabbath; He *commands* it.

> Sabbath is God's secret ingredient that He gives you to help you be successful and stay successful.

The Practice of Sabbath

Let's dive in to the practice of Sabbath, and how it can build you stronger and help you go farther faster. I will take you through the sequence of how God built Sabbath to intersect with our rhythm of living and working. Now, I want to preach at you. You need this, more than you may realize. So far in this book, I have been pushing you to do hard work, to be disciplined. In order for you to keep passion levels high, you need huge amounts of energy. Sabbath creates this like nothing else. I am willing to bet you do not honor Sabbath in your life as you should. All of us need to re-visit and re-evaluate this crucial ingredient. So, listen up and pay attention. I'm your coach. I am here to help you overcome your struggle.

1. Resist

What leads to a good Sabbath is a good work out. Just like we work out muscles in the gym with resistance training, we are working out muscles around the weak areas of our life through resistance training. This is a perfect analogy for all of us who are pushing ourselves to say no to temptations we will face in our struggle. We are re-training our mindset, and we are practicing new, healthy habits. At the same time, we are resisting bad habits that were attributing to our struggle. In doing this, we are building up high fences in our lives. We are doing strength training when we do resistance training. All hard work, for sure.

My parents both taught me a healthy work ethic. They taught me the principle of working hard, and then celebrating your work. I remember my dad saying to me "when you have worked hard doing the right things, it makes your day off that much more rewarding." When people do not put the hard work in, they will not fully enjoy the Sabbath. When people skip steps and cut corners, they cheat themselves. Rest does not fully take it's affect if you have not applied yourself and exerted energy. So, make sure you are pushing yourself hard, until "fail." Give it all you got. Leave it all on the field.

2. Retire

I love this word. When I was younger, working long hours and pushing hard, I would sometimes wish I could be an old person and just retire. No pressure, no responsibility. As I have aged, I have learned to appreciate and invest in my health. I have also learned through studying this principle of Sabbath, that I could "retire" now. Even with working in my career, I could retire and enjoy everything in life I dreamed of! True!

Retire does not just mean getting old and not working. Retire can also mean:

to withdraw to or from a particular place

www.dictionary.com

Have you ever felt like escaping? Leaving? Giving up?

I feel that way every once in a while. I think all of us do. Is that bad? I thought we are supposed to suck it up and not give up. What about that toughness mindset that I have been talking about?

The great thing about retiring is that you give yourself permission to escape. Not forever...not permanently; just every once in a while, when you need it. In fact, if you observe the Sabbath, you can retire and escape your pressure and responsibility every seventh day! How awesome!

Getting to leave and withdraw from expectations and problems is freeing. It does something psychologically to your mind that you need to feel – *release*. You need to be able to release all that you are carrying. Temptation comes when you get so weary from the weight you carry that you actually entertain the thought of leaving permanently. You think you have to make a permanent cut from your job, or, God-forbid your marriage or family to get relief from the pressure that you feel. That is an un-healthy escape, for sure. What I am talking about are regular breaks when you can withdraw so you can feel relief. You will actually be able to feel again!

> You need to be able to release all that you are carrying.

The problem we face is that on our day off, we stay in the same place where our work and responsibilities are. If we are home, we see laundry, bills, and our to-do list pilling up, staring us in the face. If we do all of our grocery shopping and errands on our day off, we really just did a different kind of work from that of our career. If we are a student, our homework lives on our computer and our social life on our smart phone, always one click away. We end up spending off time stuck in technology.

Retiring means that you withdraw to a particular place. A particular place for you. What you need to do to prepare for your Sabbath is to *prepare a place*. You get to actually pick a place close by you want to travel away to. Or, you can design a particular place in your home that is away from view of work. How fun! You get to dream up places and venues that you love and actually prepare them. This is not work to you. This is fun!

> What you need to do to prepare for your Sabbath is to *prepare a place.*

Your particular place does not need to be expensive. Your place does not need to be extravagant. It can be a coffee shop nearby where you can sit in a corner and hide. It can be at the beach, or at a park. Your place can be a long walk around your neighborhood. Your place can even be at home. It can be your back yard, or a sitting room. The key to having a place at home, however, is that you make sure to *prepare* a place. This place needs to be fixed up, cleaned up, and dressed up. Remove clutter. Make it comfortable. Find a place with a good view of nature. Or, put up art work and pictures that lift your spirits and calm your mind. If you like music, put some music on.

This place is somewhere you can escape to so you can be alone. It is a place that is set exactly as you would wish. Sometimes, you can share this space with your spouse and family. Other times, you are going to need time just by yourself. It is in these unhurried times where you will begin to feel the weight of responsibility fall off your shoulders. Only when you go to this place regularly will you begin to feel again. And, you don't have to wait until just the seventh day of Sabbath to enjoy this! You can visit this place throughout the week. You control your schedule. You are in charge of you – remember?

Plan time for your place. And, to add variety, create several places. Below is a list of places I have created, including the activities I do when at that place. Be warned, my places may not be the places that you would necessarily pick. The key is knowing what feels like a healthy escape for you. What helps you escape so you can dis-connect from the world and from responsibility? Here are mine:

Place	Time	Description
Living room	Monday and Friday mornings – 6:30 AM	I read, pray, write, listen to instrumental piano and guitar, share time with my wife after I have had time alone
Walk around my neighborhood	Every day, morning or evening	I listen to podcasts, or have silence. I think and pray as I get physical exercise. I go to the gym 3 times a week as well.
Walk around my church	Tuesday & Thursday mornings 8:15 AM – 8:45 AM	Our church campus in Stuart, FL is beautiful. After I drop my son off at the nearby school, I walk the campus and pray before I go to the office and start working.
Back yard	Monday & Friday morning or evenings in the cool months	I have a comfortable sitting area with fire pit, flowers, and pretty scenery. I will put music on and watch the fire, my favorite!

VACATION MEANS VACATE

While a regular place is essential to retire nearby home base, taking vacation is essential. I have struggled with vacations, honestly for a couple of reasons. First, I never feel I can afford them financially. I am always trying to improve our financial situation by aggressively paying off debt, and by saving and investing for the future. Secondly, I figure I can relax just as much at home as I can somewhere else. I love to be home and love my familiar surroundings.

So, travel does not peak my interest as it does other people. You may not have these issues, so you can skip along to the next section. However, if you are like me and tend to forgo vacating for a vacation, let me share what I have learned on the importance of vacating for your vacation.

The main reason we need to vacation away is for the psychological effect of helping us feel that we are escaping and retiring from responsibilities. Out of sight, out of mind. When we leave our normal surroundings and travel to a new place, it gives us a new vantage point. Seeing new places opens up our perspective to fresh insights and new feelings. When we travel to a new place, we do not feel the weight of responsibility to produce or problem solve. We simply can observe, experience and enjoy!

VISITING FAMILY WITH FAMILY

Traditionally, most of us use all of our vacation time to visit family out of state. And, we take our family with us on the visit. While this is good to do, we all know that this is not usually very restful for us. Family issues are always brewing. You are having to serve others. You are having to give up your preferences for others. The big joke we all have after a family vacation is "I need a vacation from my vacation." Taking time off work to visit family is a good thing to do. It is necessary to serve your family. We should enjoy being with our family. We should be intentional about creating memories with those we love the most. However, I am advocating that you need to *also* plan a vacation for *you* as well!

What I have learned is that I need some time away, even away from family. My wife and kids understand the pressure I carry, and they allow me to do this. Here are three trips I plan every year that fill my tank:

Trips	People	Activities
1.	Trip nearby with my dad	Walk the beach, shop, see a movie, read, eat at restaurants, catch up on sleep, great conversations with my dad
2.	Trip nearby with friends	Eat, watch movies, shop, play games, shoot guns, great conversations with my friends around a firepit
3.	Trip to West Virginia with my father-in-law	Walk trails, visit a church, read and write, enjoy the change of season, enjoy time with my father-in-law and his friends

On these trips, I am able to plan fun activities that excite me. I am able to create space to spend time alone by myself, and some time with friends I am with. I go to places where nature can be viewed and experienced. I rest physically, emotionally and spiritually. I fill up relationally with people with whom I love and trust. I produce nothing. I enjoy everything.

This creates a healthy escape where I can fill up. It is in these environments when God speaks clearly to me. I spend a lot of time seeking Him, and He never disappoints. I have journals full of what God has shared with me. I have audio recordings of piano songs I have written. I have books I have read and book ideas I have written. Vacating to these places and spaces have contributed to me being fruitful and staying fruitful!

Notice that I do not take trips alone by myself. This points back to my chapter dealing with building fences and allowing people to "parent" me. I have made a rule that I will never travel alone. I do not trust myself. Remember that we need to retire because we are tired. We have been resisting and laboring. It is when we are tired that we will struggle to resist. So, I always travel with trusted family like my dad or my father-in-law. Or, I travel with men that are close friends. I can be myself around them, yet I know they care too much about me to allow me to do anything that would be unhealthy. They would never let me jeopardize the blessings of my family and my calling by God. I can create plenty of alone-time on these trips, with my trusted men keeping a watchful eye over me.

When I come back home from one of these trips, my family notices a difference in me. My colleagues at work notice. My work improves. My attitude is positive. I have passion and energy. Ideas and insights flow out of me because I am re-charged and replenished. My family has learned to appreciate the rhythm of retiring that I need, because what I have to give to them is better. I can love them and serve them from a place of joy and passion. My church family appreciates that I keep myself healthy, so staff and volunteers gladly cover my responsibilities while I am away.

See how great retirement can be? You can retire now! Don't feel guilty about preparing a particular place where you can withdraw. You need to get your calendar out and begin planning a time to escape. As soon as you plan and confirm your vacation away with a friend or family member, you will instantly be charged with energy. Why? Anticipation! You actually re-create the Christmas affect. You have something exciting to look forward to. You have prepared a gift for yourself!

3. Rest

I covered some of the concept of rest in the section above. However, I want to point to a few key insights that I believe will help you. I have had to learn how to rest. You likely need to learn as well. Why is it so difficult for us to rest well? What keeps us from resting?

NOT ENOUGH TIME

I have a sense of urgency. That has helped me rise in leadership because I have a propensity to drive objectives forward without hesitation. The dark side of having urgency is, I tend to drive forward with everything, every day. I never feel like I have enough time to accomplish all that I want to or need to. When I am resting, I will have moments that I feel I need to produce something. I feel as if I am wasting precious time. One study I did on my unique gifts labeled me a *maximizer*. I like to improve people and things. I cannot stand good enough. I like great. I like better.

In order to rest properly, I have had to learn to deny this natural inclination to produce, to make things better. The word Sabbath commands us to rest. It also commands that labor and production are not allowed. This is shown when God produced creation in six days, and on the seventh, He rested. He stopped producing. It was not that God was tired. Rather, He was systematic. He was creating an order of how He designed life to flow for us. He created the world in a detailed sequence. After creating His crown achievement, making man and woman in His own image, God then chose to stop and rest. We must follow God's systematic flow of life and rest, and that means resisting the hurried pace of producing and accomplishing. That means you have to give yourself permission to stop and rest. Enjoy the time and relax!

When we obey God by resting and not producing or accomplishing, we make some powerful declarations:

1. God's timing is perfect, so we have plenty of time to stop and rest and get done what we need to accomplish

2. We will accomplish what *God wants us to accomplish* when we put Him first by honoring the Sabbath day

3. When we honor God's system of Sabbath, we will accomplish more than we could on our own, because God will honor us and bless our work

You have enough time. You have plenty of time. My Pastor, Todd Mullins says something that reminds us that God's timing is perfect:

"God can do more in seconds that it would take us centuries to accomplish"

NOT ENOUGH RESOURCES

Another struggle I grapple with is not feeling like I have enough resources. Therefore, I tend to earn more money, more resources, more opportunity. I can easily overcommit myself, and have been guilty of taking on work at the expense of not resting. It does not matter how much money I earn or how much success I acquire. I always feel like there is more that I need. I am a maximizer, remember? Always better. Never enough.

Not having enough is a mindset which is pervasive in society today. People work seven days a week. Having a side hustle is commonplace today. Both the husband and the wife have full blown careers, because they believe that they need a certain level of income. While there is nothing wrong with hustling and working hard to build a successful career, too many of us are working too many hours from a sense of fear. Sabbath rest happens when we have a sense of faith.

> # Sabbath rest happens when we have a sense of faith.

Honoring Sabbath does not promise that you will have everything you want. But God promises that He will provide everything you need. There is a difference. Taking a day to rest makes a powerful declaration:

I have faith that God will provide everything I need

The writer of the book of Psalms, King David, made this statement:

> The Lord is my Shepherd. I have all that I need.
> He makes me lie down in green pastures. He
> leads me beside still waters. He restores my soul.
> Psalm 23

He makes me. Sabbath is God's command for you. But God's commands are to bless you, not to hurt you. God is saying to you: *Come ye yourselves apart and rest awhile (Mark 6:31). Watch as I provide for you.*

The reason we struggle with resting while there is more work to be done and opportunities to seize is because we feel we must be working! It takes us hustling and laboring. If you want something done, do it yourself. However, honoring Sabbath forces us to sit and watch.

Watch God *produce* for you.

Watch God *provide* for you.

In the Bible, one name that describes God is *Jehovah Jireh: The One Who provides*. When God produces, it is effortless for Him. When God provides, it comes from His unlimited resources. He has untold riches and treasures. God is the one that provides you with opportunity. God opens doors and God closes them. You and I need to realize that God will provide all of the resources we need. When you honor Him by observing the Sabbath, He will make sure you have opportunities. You see, God wants you to enjoy your work. He doesn't want you to be burdened by it. Without God, it seems we will never have enough. With God, we will have more than enough.

I AM NOT ENOUGH

When we come to the realization that we do not have enough time or enough resources, we realize the real truth: **we are not enough**. We lack the wisdom, the relationships, and the pedigree. We lack the strategy, the opportunities and the skills. Once we admit that we are not enough, we can acknowledge that we are in great need of God. Sabbath acknowledges our need for God.

Jesus says this to you:

> I am the vine; you are the branches. If you remain in me and I in you, you will bear much fruit; apart from me you can do nothing.
> John 15:5 NIV

It takes humility and vulnerability to admit that you are not enough. Yet, when you arrive at that conclusion, you will be free. Your burden becomes light. As soon as you choose to put your trust and faith in Jesus, you now become connected to Him, the "Vine." He becomes your friend. He becomes your Source. He becomes your Savior and your Lord. Now, He becomes the leader in your life. And, He will never lead you wrong. He will make sure you produce much fruit! He will open doors that otherwise would seem impossible.

Jesus will fill you with wisdom, strength, ideas, and passion. He will feed you and fill you. He will work in your life and will work through your life, to bring great impact to the world! With this in mind, you can truly trust and rest on the Sabbath. You can trust God while you work. And You can rest while God works!

> You can trust God while you work. And You can rest while God works!

4. Renew

Once we rest, we begin to re-gain energy to do something very healing. That is, we begin to renew.

> ...but those who hope in the LORD will renew
> their strength. They will soar on wings like
> eagles; they will run and not grow weary, they
> will walk and not be faint.
> Isaiah 40:31 NIV

Other versions of this famous passage of scripture say it this way:

They who **wait** on the LORD...

Those who **trust** in the LORD...

Resting is waiting. It is trusting. Resting is living with a hope that God is up to something awesome for your life. And, when you rest well, you will begin to renew.

You see, life is a battle. You and I forget that what we do every day is tough. Those helpful seven are downright awful. You are fighting attack, temptation, criticism, adversity, and disappointments. And while these can be used to toughen you up, they also wear you down. You come out of a tough day or a tough week bruised and scraped. Your emotions are damaged. Your spirit grows weary. Your confidence is compromised. Your body is tired. You have been bent out of shape and zapped of all of your passion. Solving problems has left you fatigued. What you need to do is to renew.

I love that scripture verse in the book of Isaiah. You were designed to be an eagle.

*You were made to **soar** above your circumstances*

*You were made to **run** with your dreams*

*You were made to **walk** in to your destiny*

When we renew ourselves, we restore ourselves to the optimal, original position God intended for us. We must be aware of our condition every day to evaluate what needs to be renewed in us. As we learn more about our unique make up as individuals, we can more accurately do activities that renew us. What renews you? It is different for everyone.

If you are an extrovert personality, you likely need social activity with family and friends. Game night and social gatherings fill your tank.

If you are introverted, you likely need lots of space away from people and noise. You need silence to hear yourself think. You need to hide away to re-charge.

If you are competitive, you need something to challenge you.

If you are curious, you need something new and exciting to explore and learn about.

When you learn your uniqueness, you realize that you need activities that reinforce who you are. To be successful in life, you must learn to bend and adapt. But doing this all week makes us feel bent out of shape. Doing activities that invigorate you will put you back into shape, the shape God designed you to be.

> # Doing activities that invigorate you will put you back into shape, the shape God designed you to be.

For me, I need to rest and relax. I like to read, write, pray and sit and "veg." Then, I like to exercise by walking and going to the gym. When I am feeling more energetic, what renews me is actually washing cars and cleaning house. I know that sounds crazy! That may feel like work to you. But to me, it is renewing.

Remember that I am a maximizer, meaning I like to improve things. So, I like to clean, organize, polish, and scrub. I like my shirts ironed and ready all hung neatly in my closet. I like my shoes polished. Having a clean house, a shiny car and clothes pressed makes me feel prepared for the week. When I am prepared, I feel proud. And, I have scratched the itch that I have accomplished something. Then, I reward myself with more rest and some good food. I literally will walk around the house later that night and view all of my accomplishments with pride and say, like God did after his creation: "it is good."

Now, I know that this may sound hypocritical to accomplish something with doing work. But notice that this comes only after a lot of rest. This comes after good sleep, much rest, reading, praying, quiet in retirement in my particular place. I do not do chores that feel like work to me. I do activities, rather that I enjoy. Chores are a have-to. Activities are a get-to. The point I am making is that I know what renews me. These activities may not renew you. Similarly, other activities that renew you do not renew me:

- Some of my friends like to hunt. Not for me. Too much sweating.
- Others like the beach. Not for me. Too much sun and bugs.
- Others like going to the city. Not for me. Too expensive and too much traffic.
- Some like to watch a sports game. Not me. I get bored.
- Some like having friends over their home for a party. Not for me. I like my privacy in my house. Too much cleanup of the house I just polished.

No judgement on them. If that renews them, then great! Don't judge me. I have my weird quirks. But they renew me. I have many other little quirky things I do within my regimen as well. And, as I find other interests, I add them in. It is fun to stay curious and to explore. You learn about yourself. You continue to explore parts of you that you did not know were there. That is what keeps your passion vibrant. That is what keeps you soaring, running and walking!

One other insight I have learned. The activities I find myself drawn to for renewal are quite opposite of what I do in my work. I love my work. I feel I am good at what I get to do for my profession. I am a pastor. So, I am caring for people. Not surprisingly, on my day off, I do not want to be with people. Crazy, I know. Because I enjoy people very much. However, doing physical chores and working out in the gym renew me. What I have noticed is that when I do a task at home, I get to do it by myself. I can control the outcome without having to help another person process. It does not require my patience to listen and compromise. I do not have to lead people toward a common goal. All I get to do is make something better on my own time in my own way. When I walk to the gym, I feel like I am making progress. I am literally moving forward.

What are those "opposite tasks" that may help to offset what you do for work? What are activities that use another part of your brain? Take a moment to write out a few. Experiment. There are hobbies and tasks that you can apply yourself to that will actually renew your spirit, mind and body for the next day of work.

5. Reward

Celebration is so important. Many business studies have pointed to team success based on how well the leader celebrates the team when they accomplish something great. They came to this conclusion because they understand this powerful principle:

What is rewarded is repeated

If you have never heard that before, it probably jumped off the page. If you have heard that, you probably need to hear it again. Most of us do not take enough time to celebrate ourselves or celebrate others. At best, we give a quick nod of congratulations and move on to the next challenge. This is due to our fast-paced conditioning and our impatience to conquer the next big thing.

If you want to reach your goal of overcoming your struggle, you need to celebrate the wins. It is not about having pride or about just enjoying the moment. It is understanding that rewards re-invigorate your confidence. They energize your passion. Stopping to truly celebrate a small win blows fresh wind in your sail to propel you toward a bigger win.

> CELEBRATING A SMALL WIN BLOWS FRESH WIND IN YOUR SAIL TO PROPEL YOU TOWARD A BIGGER WIN.

Whenever I talk with people who share their struggle with me, I notice that they all have a common body language. Their shoulders are slumped, their head is down, and they can hardly look me in the eye. Their voice is low in tone and broken, revealing low confidence. They tell me how bad they are and how ashamed they feel. They are so beaten down and overwhelmed with their struggle.

After I let them express themselves, I begin to build them up. I do this by celebrating what they have done good in their life. If they have come to church, I will celebrate that. The fact that they have come up to a pastor asking for help is a huge step, so I will affirm their courage and humility. I look for aspects of their life that they have done well and begin to point out how awesome they are. I point to where they are winning, even if small wins. Why do I do this? I will tell you why.

When I show the person where they are winning, I am building them back up. Helping them to see how they are winning will reinforce that same action. When I celebrate them, I am not just making them feel better, I am saying to them *do more of that. That is good.* These people have been beating themselves up badly. And, the people they have hurt by the consequences of their struggle have been adding to their pain. These people are in dire need of a trusted pastor to pull them up, love them and accept them where they are.

The quickest way to do this is to affirm some good in their life. They have been so focused on their struggle that they have forgotten their success. Everybody has something they can point to that is successful. They have simply forgotten. A pastor looks for the success and reminds the person of it. They celebrate it with them, so that the person can have permission to celebrate it. What happens when a person is celebrated? What does it feel like to be affirmed? It is like wind in your sails. It is like ointment to a wound.

Before I even begin to address the struggle, I point to some success. Nothing in their life has changed. However, their body language does. Their head lifts up. They look me in the eye. Their shoulders pull back. They stand up straighter. Their voice gets louder, and their words move more quickly.

Once I have loved them and then celebrated them, I can then give them some next steps to begin tackling the struggle they are dealing with. I speak my confidence in to them. I declare God's destiny over them. I pray that God's Spirit of strength and presence will fill them. Then, I send them off to begin their journey to overcoming their struggle. As a Pastor, I have been privileged to see hundreds of men and women heal, grow and develop their lives so they are empowered to overcome their struggle. Our church is filled with them. I love it! It was not me who did it. With God's help, it was the individual who took the necessary steps. They had the courage and focus to apply themselves fully to the process of healing and health. My part was that of a faithful Pastor.

Listen ➤ Love ➤ Celebrate ➤ Guide ➤ Support

You see, we all too often struggle with rewarding ourselves because we do not feel that we win very often. One step forward and two steps back. We feel that if we do not have a perfect record of overcoming our struggle, we have failed. We think that because we have not made huge progress, we do not deserve to reward ourselves. And, it does not help to see someone else's success in the area that we struggle.

I heard Television personality and Comedian, Steve Harvey share about his struggle. He had many struggles early in his life. He stuttered, hardly being able to carry a conversation. He was also poor. At the start of his career, he was homeless. His story of overcoming is motivational. Steve Harvey shared this great insight:

> DON'T COMPARE YOUR SUCCESS BY HOW YOU MEASURE UP TO OTHERS COMPARE YOUR SUCCESS BY HOW FAR YOU HAVE COME

What a great thought! When we remember where we have come from, and then measure our overall progress, we will have a lot to celebrate! That deserves a reward. What is the use of working and pushing if we do not enjoy our success?

I have had to grow in this area. My mother has had to get a hold of me sometimes when I start sharing some of the bigger challenges I want to conquer. She will coach me: "Learn to be satisfied with what you have accomplished. Stop and enjoy it." That has helped me when I get spun up.

Think of some successes in your life that you do not give yourself enough credit for. You need to reward yourself today for some of these un-celebrated successes:

- You have stayed married
- You have loved and supported your children
- You have stayed in school
- You have stayed in your job
- You may not have a job, but you are still looking for one
- You are paying the bills
- You are serving people in some way

If you can't celebrate one of the above, what are some other wins you can celebrate?

It's important to point out the success in your life and reward yourself. Rewarding yourself will give you the lift to reach for the next success!

6. Remember

And remember that you were a slave in the land of Egypt, and the Lord your God brought you out from there by a mighty hand and by an outstretched arm; therefore the Lord your God commanded you to keep the Sabbath day.
Deuteronomy 5:14 NKJV

Going back to that scripture in the book of Deuteronomy shows us another important element of honoring the Sabbath. God wants us to *remember.*

We have a short term memory. We take our benefits and gifts for granted. When we forget how we got to where we are, we can let pride creep up. We can all too easily begin to think that it is our hard work, skill and wisdom that produced all that we enjoy in life.

The Jewish people were gifted. Industrious. Insightful and creative. They were God's Chosen People, and God had blessed them immensely. However, just like children can tend to do, they would have short term memory loss remembering where they came from. They had been slaves in Egypt. They owned nothing. They had no skills, except to make building blocks made of straw. Years later, God delivered them out of slavery, and led them to a beautiful land "flowing with milk and honey."

God wanted them to remember their humble beginnings so that they would appreciate His mighty salvation and great provision. Why? Because when we forget where we came from, we soon stop appreciating it. Lack of appreciation breeds discontent.

Do you appreciate what you have? Think of all of the things you have in your life. It probably doesn't take you long to run through a list of images in your head of all that you. A house, vehicles, clothes, furniture, sports equipment, technology. Think through your finances, your assets. Think through how many shoes you have (ahh, I caught you. You have more than you probably could count!)

At some point, you stop listing your material things and begin to realize that your most valuable "things" are your family. Friends. It is your relationships that should matter most to you. How do you put a value on that? More costly than any amount of money!

How about your health? Your gifts that God has given you? What about the gift of time? How about where you live? Your career? Are you thankful for your calling? For your ability to create? To gain wisdom and insight? Do you appreciate your ability to choose? Are you thankful for living in your country?

Now, after rehearsing this massive list of "things" in your life, how do you feel? Do you feel blessed? Or burdened? I would put money on the fact that you feel BLESSED. I would imagine that you feel you are overflowing in blessings! More than you deserve. Now, compare those to your problems. Your irritations in life. ....they seem pretty small right now, don't they? That's what happens when we take time to remember all that God has blessed us with!

REMEMBER GOD

As we take time to remember our blessings, we should not dare leave out God. For, it is God that has given us these many blessings. He is the reason we are blessed.

When we remember God, we put our focus back on Him. Let's be careful not to spend more time on the blessings than we do the One who gives the blessings! The biggest blessing is not what He gives, it is who He is.

Of all of the benefits the Sabbath bring us, the greatest by far is getting to spend time pondering who God is. All of the other benefits of retire, rest, reflect, and reward allow us to do that which fills our lives more than anything else. That is, fill our lives with God's presence.

THE GLORY OF GOD

When we take our focus off the things in our life, and put it on the giver of all good things, we see something that is far greater than any "thing" we could ever hope for or ask for. God's glory. God alone is more beautiful, more magnificent than anything we think we could want or think we need. Sabbath makes us remember that God is enough. He is more than enough. We ought to seek His glory. We will see His glory when we experience His presence. Look at this interaction between Moses and God in the book of Exodus:

> We will see His glory when we experience His presence.

Moses said to the Lord, "You have been telling me, 'Lead these people,' but you have not let me know whom you will send with me. You have said, 'I know you by name and you have found favor with me.' If you are pleased with me, teach me your ways so I may know you and continue to find favor with you. Remember that this nation is your people."
The Lord replied, "My Presence will go with you, and I will give you rest."
Then Moses said to him, "If your Presence does not go with us, do not send us up from here. How will anyone know that you are pleased with me and with your people unless you go with us? What else will distinguish me and your people from all the other people on the face of the earth?"

And the Lord said to Moses, "I will do the very thing you have asked, because I am pleased with you and I know you by name."
Then Moses said, "Now show me your glory."
And the Lord said, "I will cause all my goodness to pass in front of you, and I will proclaim my name, the Lord, in your presence. I will have mercy on whom I will have mercy, and I will have compassion on whom I will have compassion. But," he said, "you cannot see my face, for no one may see me and live."
Then the Lord said, "There is a place near me where you may stand on a rock. When my glory passes by, I will put you in a cleft in the rock and cover you with my hand until I have passed by. Then I will remove my hand and you will see my back; but my face must not be seen."

Exodus 33:12-23 New International Version (NIV)

This conversation is familiar, isn't it? It should be. Do you see yourself in the story? Can you relate to Moses? You and I, like Moses feel a heavy weight of responsibility on our shoulders. We are between a rock and a hard place. Work and home. One project versus another. Your boss, your employees. Opportunity and family. Health and habits. So, when we are praying to God, we feel the need to explain the tensions we manage in our life ....as if He does not quite get it. ....as if He does not see all that we see.

Moses is trying to explain his challenges with Israel to God. I love how Moses even tries to put pressure back on God by reminding Him *these are your people, God!* Ha! My wife has accused me of throwing that on her when I am feeling bothered with responsibility in our home. When I arrive home from work, I will ask "what are we going to do about dinner?" She will respond "I don't know. What do you have planned? I work outside the home too. I serve in our church too. Is it always up to me to take all of the responsibility at home?" Fair comeback, I must admit. ....let's order pizza.

Moses at least did one thing right. That is, He talked with God. The Bible says that Moses talked with God, as one friend talks with another. (Exodus 33:11) Moses nurtured a close relationship with God. Though Moses came from a place of stress and fear, at least He approached God. Notice how God meets Him where He is at. God promises Moses:

> "My Presence will go with you, and I will give you rest."

When we are in the very presence of God, we will experience rest. True rest can fill our lives even in the midst of trouble and strife. True rest can be ours in the midst of busyness and fast-paced seasons. True rest can be experienced in the waiting for answers and clarity. When we are in the presence of God, we can rest no matter what is happening around us. We are safe!

Moses loved being in the presence of God. He had close relationship with God, having walked closely with Him through the journey to Egypt and leading the people out

---

God desires to show more of Who He is to those who desire more of Him.

---

of Egypt. Moses desired to know more about God. Moses wanted to see God, in all of His glory and beauty. One would think that Moses was so audacious as to think He could ask to see God's glory. Yet, God obliged. Why? Because God desires to show more of Who He is to those who desire more of Him. God responded to Moses:

> **"I will cause all my goodness to pass in front of you, and I will proclaim my name, the Lord, in your presence."**

Moses had a tough assignment: lead slaves in the wilderness with no food or water for 40 years. Teach them God's law and lead them to the promised land. All by faith, according to God's direction. If you have ever had to lead people toward an objective, you understand that leadership can be lonely. Responsibility can feel heavy. Faith can feel hopeless. Moses needed constant encouragement. He needed to remember that God had called Him and had provided for Him. God would show Moses His beauty and great glory. God would proclaim His Name to remind Moses that God was with him.

Remembering on the Sabbath helps you spend time in God's presence. You can thank God for all He has given you, both small things and big things. You can worship Him, reminding yourself to focus more on the Giver of the blessings than the blessings themselves. Spend time in God's presence as often as you can. You will realize that the cares of this world will pale in comparison to experiencing the glory of God!

Conclusion

See why the Sabbath is your secret ingredient to staying strong and sustaining for the long term over your struggle? It is powerful in re-charging you. Honoring the Sabbath once a week for 24 hours and even in short zones throughout the week will keep you rejuvenated and refreshed.

The order I prescribe to celebrate and honor the Sabbath in your life follows the sequence below:

1. **Resist**	Great rest is enjoyed after doing great work
2. **Retire**	Create a place to withdraw
3. **Rest**	Release control and rest by faith
4. **Renew**	Do activities that invigorate you back in to shape
5. **Reward**	Celebrating small wins motivate you toward bigger wins
6. **Remember**	Remembering your blessings points you to the Giver

Let me urge you: don't feel guilty about enjoying the Sabbath. Have you noticed how I have been changing my use of verb from *commanding* to *enjoying*? God commands it **because** He wants you to enjoy it! Your struggle has been beating you down. And while it is going to take a lot of work to pre-program your mind and discipline your life, the Sabbath is the "magic pill" God has given you to strengthen your resolve and overcome.

Give the Sabbath a lot of time and thought. Begin blocking out your calendar for ample time to focus yourself on enjoying it. It will give life to your soul and strength to your body!

Jesus shares the heart of God for us. I have included two versions of the same scripture passage below. Both share such great imagery that can show the joy and rest we can experience *in* God and *with* God:

Come to me, all you who are weary and burdened, and I will give you rest. Take my yoke upon you and learn from me, for I am gentle and humble in heart, and you will find rest for your souls. For my yoke is easy and my burden is light.
Matthew 11:28-30 NIV

Are you tired? Worn out? Burned out on religion? Come to me. Get away with me and you'll recover your life. I'll show you how to take a real rest. Walk with me and work with me— watch how I do it. Learn the unforced rhythms of grace. I won't lay anything heavy or ill-fitting on you. Keep company with me and you'll learn to live freely and lightly.
Matthew 11:28-30 The Message

Chapter 9

Ready for More

Thus far, I have showed you how you can overcome your struggle. I have pointed you toward the tools that will lead to health and strength. So, what next? What do you do once you achieve a level of health and victory? What is the deeper meaning behind getting healthy and strong?

Of course, the obvious answer is to find freedom. If you struggle with anxiety, your win is having peace. If you struggle with not being able to find friends, your win is learning how to be a good friend so you can have good friends. If yours is a physical struggle of some sort, your win is learning how to live a vibrant and purposeful life in the midst of managing that physical struggle.

The greater meaning that I want to pose is that you are now ***ready for more.*** More what? ***More.***

When you finally reach that beautiful place of freedom and victory over your struggle, celebrate! I congratulate you! Well done! I am proud of you! You have effectively lived out the process of work, rest, and reward that I have coached in this book. And, you are enjoying the full life that is now possible. Now, I want to show you how you are set up to achieve greater significance and impact through your own victory. *(this is where it gets really good...)*

A Set Up

The level of success you have achieved is really just a set up for now greater achievements God has in store for you. I want you to begin to look at the health and success you now have as God has invested in you. What? you ask. I did all of this work, not God! OK, I get it. I know you did all of the work. But God is the one Who strengthened you and supported you through this. God was patient with you and me while we were working on personal growth in our life. Now, God expects more from us. Take a look at this kingdom principle Jesus teaches us on how we invest that which God has given us:

Again, the Kingdom of Heaven can be illustrated by the story of a man going on a long trip. He called together his servants and entrusted his money to them while he was gone. He gave five bags of silver to one, two bags of silver to another, and one bag of silver to the last— dividing it in proportion to their abilities. He then left on his trip.
The servant who received the five bags of silver began to invest the money and earned five more. The servant with two bags of silver also went to work and earned two more. But the servant who received the one bag of silver dug a hole in the ground and hid the master's money. After a long time their master returned from his trip and called them to give an account of how they had used his money. The servant to whom he had entrusted the five bags of silver came forward with five more and said, 'Master, you gave me five bags of silver to invest, and I have earned five more.'

The master was full of praise. 'Well done, my good and faithful servant. You have been faithful in handling this small amount, so now I will give you many more responsibilities. Let's celebrate together!'

The servant who had received the two bags of silver came forward and said, 'Master, you gave me two bags of silver to invest, and I have earned two more.'

The master said, 'Well done, my good and faithful servant. You have been faithful in handling this small amount, so now I will give you many more responsibilities. Let's celebrate together!'

Then the servant with the one bag of silver came and said, 'Master, I knew you were a harsh man, harvesting crops you didn't plant and gathering crops you didn't cultivate. I was afraid I would lose your money, so I hid it in the earth. Look, here is your money back.'

But the master replied, 'You wicked and lazy servant! If you knew I harvested crops I didn't plant and gathered crops I didn't cultivate, why didn't you deposit my money in the bank? At least I could have gotten some interest on it.'

Then he ordered, 'Take the money from this servant, and give it to the one with the ten bags of silver. To those who use well what they are given, even more will be given, and they will have an abundance. But from those who do nothing, even what little they have will be taken away. Now throw this useless servant into

outer darkness, where there will be weeping and
gnashing of teeth.'
Matthew 25:14-30 New Living Translation

Wow. That last part...weeping and gnashing of teeth...too
gruesome.

What is the moral of the story? God expects more from
us. He expects more from me. He expects more from you.
We cannot stay satisfied simply enjoying the success and
freedom God has helped us achieve. We must invest what
we have been given, so it can multiply and become greater.

The reason I am making this point is because we live in a
narcissistic culture. We always tend to think of ourselves
first and foremost. That is human nature. I see many
people who go to the gym, focus on their savings account,
are active in their Bible study group. But that is it. They
have a healthy marriage, and their children are well-
behaved. Their home is perfectly organized and clean.
Their Social Media posts show a happy life. While life is
to be celebrated, I wonder how much they are affecting the
world around them? Who else are they helping? What else
are they carrying to serve someone else?

Our churches today have learned how to effectively engage
our people to connect so that they can grow spiritually.
Understanding people's busy schedules, churches have
learned how to help people connect, grow and serve in a
more convenient way. We have shortened church services
to one hour. We have created missions projects that last a
couple of hours, where people are given a t-shirt, tools and
snacks for when they serve. People can join a group that
is close to their home. We even have posted our messages
online so people have 24 hour availability to watch in their
time frame. I am a Pastor, and I do all of these things,
because I want to help people connect, grow and serve in
our church. It makes sense.

One of the unintended outcomes of making church convenient is that people may take church for granted. They begin to take or leave what the church offers as it fits their schedule. My fear is that people lose the sense of urgency and personal responsibility to BE the church, without the prompting and "spoon-feeding" of the Pastor.

My heart for people is that they step out in faith into new, uncharted territory that God is calling them to. My desire is for people to actually begin to create their own opportunities to serve. I want people to hunger for the presence of God and the Word of God during the week, not just every other week when they catch a service at church or online. *God has more ready for them!*

The great news is that I see many people stepping out by faith in our church to BE the church and to BUILD *their* church. Our people take personal ownership of the ministries. They steward the heart and mission of their church. I hear stories of people inviting friends and neighbors to join them for church. I hear stories of men's groups finding a single mom and deciding to take a collection to help with expenses. I see examples of Godly people in our church intentionally mentoring others in the church, to help them grow. Love our church!

Invested

The "talent" mentioned in the parable Jesus taught equated to a large amount of money. Funny to me that though the talent in ancient times described money, we know the word, talent as a natural gift. Either way, whether speaking of a great amount of money or a natural gift, the parable describes talent to mean something of great value. Three men were each given talents. However, the men demonstrated different actions with how they handled their talents. We see two contrasting attitudes in these servants:

One man had a protected posture in how he handled the talent his master gave him. The other two men had an invested posture. They realized that their master did not give them the talent. The master *entrusted* the talent to them. There is a difference of how you see what God has given you. God has given to you so that He can entrust to you.

Entrusted

I love this word. *Entrusted.* It insinuates trust has been given. Trust has been put into something else. Someone else. A gift has been given to us, but with a purpose. And, with an expectation. When we receive a gift, we can sometimes feel it is just for us to enjoy for ourselves. Certainly, gifts should be enjoyed. We should use them and find great fulfillment in them. However, we should look at the deeper meaning as to why we have been given a gift. If you have been given a talent (a natural ability), you need to stop and ask "why do I have this? And, how did I get this?" This line of questioning should lead eventually to the "*who* gave this?"

> God has given to you so that He can entrust to you.

Freely you have received; freely give.
Matthew 10: 8 NIV

Jesus sent His Disciples out to serve people. Before He sent them out, He gave them instructions. The last word Jesus shared in this passage of scripture was to remind them that He has invested in them. He wanted His Disciples to realize that He was entrusting them with the investment He had made in to them. *"Freely you have received from me. Now, freely give."* What a powerful reminder to us. God loves you. He has invested in you. He has given His presence, His wisdom and His people to support you. He has given His power and His Word. He has healed you, freed you, forgiven and cleansed you. Now, freely give. Freely give to others who are where you were.

Teach What You Have Learned

As a Star Wars fan, I loved the character, Yoda. Yoda was the little green creature who was, in fact a great Jedi Master. The Jedi were like Samurai, Ninja Warriors who fought using lightsabers and special powers. Yoda taught the hero of Star Wars, Luke Skywalker how to use the force. After extensive training, Yoda challenged Luke "pass on what you have learned."

As a young man, I was not much in to teaching others. I was learning at such a rapid pace myself, that I wanted to show everyone around how great I was. In my younger years, I was an avid student of music. I learned all I could in playing the piano. Classical, Pop, Jazz, and Gospel were all musical genres that I loved and studied. I also took an interest in leading choirs and vocal ensembles. I studied the best conductors and vocal coaches. Later, I discovered the brilliance of orchestration, writing out music for musicians and singers. This led to a love for recording in great studios. The last thing I was concerned about was helping someone else. Truth be told, I actually was trying to outdo others.

I had an internal, secret game I would play. Every time I stepped in to a room of musicians, singers, or arrangers, I would scan the room to see if there was anybody who was better than me. If I found that I was the best, a great sense of pride would fill my heart. If I found someone who was better than me, I would seek them out and learn from them. My intention was not humility, however. My motive was competition, to eventually beat and surpass them. King of the Hill, I think is what we called this in grade school. This is a horrible attitude; I admit to you. Immaturity. Insecurity. That was me in my teens and twenties. Sorry to let you down.

What was sad was that I had so many great mentors and teachers who had helped me along the way. I may have had some natural talent. But I see now that it was the piano lessons, funded by my parents. It was the church that gave me instruments and platform, led by my worship pastors and built by my father. It was the band teachers and college teachers who taught me and sharpened me.

One of the best mentors I ever had was a young college graduate who had started a traveling music group that I auditioned for when I was in Bible College. His name was Nate Carter. He had been a star student, earning him in-roads to arrange and record music professionally. Nate was a hot ticket leader and music producer who was sought after. I first met Nate when he held auditions for his music group, Frontline. I did my best to dazzle him with my keyboard skills. He hired me and invited me in his circle of students who would make up his group for the year.

I was already impressed with Nate's musical talent of songwriting and arranging. However, I was drawn to his kindness and affirmation of me and the other students in the group. Nate had a humility and authenticity about him. People loved working with Nate. Nate was an observer. He was quiet at times, noticing those around him. He noticed my talent. But he also saw my ambition and insecurity. He never judged me. Rather, He talked a lot about his walk with God, and encouraged those of us in his musical group to invest in our personal relationship with God through times of prayer and worship. I remember that.

Nate was the first person to give me a chance at music arranging. Back then, we still used pencil and paper to arrange music. This was about the time that Apple computers were coming out with music notation software. Fun times! Nate had an upcoming song we were going to record on our Frontline album. Nate came to me one day and asked "would you want to arrange this song for our group? Give it a try?" I was thrilled! A dream! I felt like I was in the big leagues. This arrangement would be recorded in a real studio with great singers and musicians! We would perform this on our next concert tour. I would be on a recording that people would listen to.

I went to my dorm room and stayed up many late nights writing and re-writing the score. I felt confident, having finished Composition and Arranging classes with the same instructor that had taught Nate years before. "Surely, my arrangement will be flawless!" I thought. A week later, when I brought it to Nate, he was gracious. However, I could tell he saw mistakes. He did not say, but I knew his observing looks as he studied my score. Using his red pencil, Nate made several edits. Not getting too discouraged, I took his edits and started over making the changes. With score sheets, you usually have to re-write the whole musical arrangement every single time. Thank God for music notation software today!

My second submission was better, but Nate still had that look on his face. And time was drawing close before rehearsals would start for the recording. More late nights ensued. However, I didn't mind. It was totally worth it. And, as I corrected, I was learning! Nate saw musical patterns and ideas that I had not fully understood. He understood, because he had worked with brass, strings, and rhythm section. He understood vocal range for singers and harmony tensions. He was a genius.

Nate continued to invest in me. He taught me everything he knew. He introduced me to his connections and hired me for future recording sessions. He invited me to co-write songs with him, some that were published and performed. Nate also invested spiritually into me. He always pointed me back to building my relationship with God.

I remember thanking Nate one day for all he had done for me. I asked him "why do you help so many of us students?" Nate paused for a moment and replied, "I get greater joy out of helping others succeed." That statement struck me. That was a new concept I had never heard before. I was only 21 years old I think when he first dropped that truth on me. I still had the rest of my twenties to feed my ambition to make a name for myself. But, that insight began to root in my spirit.

> I get greater joy out of helping others succeed.
> —Nate Carter

Greater Joy

Nate's heart to help others has become my heart. I have moved from performing music to pastoring people. My profession has changed as I have changed. I still love music. I still play piano from time to time. My musical season was full, allowing me to achieve beyond my wildest dreams. Now, I am building people. I am building churches. I am investing myself in the Treasure Coast of South Florida, by raising up men and women to pastor, lead, start ministries, businesses, run for political office and more.

I still love to accomplish great personal goals for my own life. It's not that I have just given up on myself. I have so much ambition and vision for my life! I am writing books. I have goals to record more music. I want to start ministries and companies. But, my greater joy is to see my wife succeed in her business and her calling. My greater joy is to see my daughter be beautiful, vibrant and brilliant. My greater joy is to see my son take his place of leadership in our family heritage. He is rugged. He is a warrior, smart and determined. I am proud of him.

> # When you let people rise beyond you, they always turn and point back to you.

It brings me greater joy to see my friends, my team I serve with all become who God intended them to be. I get excited when I see others preach. Others lead. Others achieve. I get pumped when I see others slay a dragon, conquer their fear, overcome their struggle. I cheer and celebrate with them. I remember all of love and support I have given them as they rise from obscurity to significance. And when I let people rise beyond me, they always turn and point back to me.

The people you invest in will forever be changed for the better. That, my friend can be a greater joy in your life. Teach what you have learned. Look around you and lift someone else up. You have come a long way in overcoming your struggle. Now, it's time to invest that which has been entrusted to you.

Show Up

Another aspect of investing the gift that God has entrusted to you is in how you lead. You may not think of yourself as a leader. Most people I interact with do not consider themselves a leader. While I understand their hesitancy to become the next Napoleon Bonaparte, I believe every person is designed to be a leader. In fact, I will take it one step farther. Every person *should be* a leader, leading in some way.

When you have found success in your life, you have something worth sharing. Something that **needs sharing!** You have real life experience, chalk full of setbacks, hurts and obstacles that you have had to deal with. You have lived through some tough pain, and you have lived beyond them! Whether you realize it or not, there are people who need to hear your story. There are people around you who need to hear from you.

Does this mean I think you need to start a video channel online? Do you need to get going on your first book? You're not a good public speaker, you say?

No, you may not be the type who enjoys posting, writing or speaking publicly. But I am challenging you to begin to lead. I am challenging you to step up. You know what leaders do? They show up.

Leaders who show up set the tone. Leaders who show up take initiative. Leaders go first. When the way in unclear, the leader goes first. When no one has a plan, the leader brings people together to create a plan. When there is no momentum in the group, the leader sparks energy and inspires the group to get going. And...the Leader always shows up.

As you have grappled with your struggle, you have likely learned this: your struggle will never win when you just keep showing up.

No matter how many times you struggle and fail, you always keep showing up. The next day, you start fresh practicing your healthy habits. The next week, you get with your mentor and your inner circle of trusted friends. The next morning, you practice right thinking and

> Your struggle will never win when you just keep showing up.

right talking. When you are discouraged, you don't allow yourself to stay home. You don't allow yourself to sulk in bed or lounge on the couch. You jack yourself up and push yourself to show up to that Celebrate Recovery meeting. You deny yourself, focusing on the joy that is set before you, as Jesus did.

Use that same tough-as-nails mentality as you begin to step into leadership. I know you are thinking "I am not ready for leadership. I have been a mess!" Well, you are already practicing self-leadership. Now is the best time to begin to lead others. And the first step to leading others is to simply to show up.

Places to Show Up

This is such a powerful teaching. I want you to really lean in to this section. Take this personally. Let me motivate you. Let me change your thinking. That is what I am trying to do through this entire book: challenge your thinking, about how you see your struggle, how you see obstacles, and how you view yourself. Maybe your problem in life has been that you have let yourself get away with too much. Maybe your parent allowed you to sit on the sidelines while they solved all of your problems. When there was conflict or pain, your mom would comfort you and try to protect you from any discomfort. Maybe your father worked so hard for your family so you would not have to experience the feeling of failure.

Many of us have been going through life as a timid by-stander. We play it safe. We choose not to engage. But, we have found that life does not allow us to sit out of the game. If we do, life happens *to* us, whether we like it or not. And, no parent, pastor, attorney or friend can lead your life. *You* have to lead *you*. You have to have a show-up-mentality to your life. You have to show up every day, in every venue. Let's explore the areas in our life that we need to show up and lead:

HOME

This is the first and most important venue we need to show up. So many of us struggle with our home life. Our family dynamic is weak and anemic. Your career may be booming. Your consistency at the gym has earned you a healthy physique. Great. But what use is success and money if your marriage is ruined? What good is physical health if your kids can't stand you? Jesus said this:

> And what do you benefit if you gain the whole world but lose your own soul?
> Mark 8:36 NLT

Your family is really an extension of you. If you are married, two have become one. If you have kids, they are your inheritance. If you are the child in the home, your parents are your caregivers and providers. Your family is supposed to be your support system, before your friends or co-workers. Your family is where you come from, who you belong to.

Our home needs to be a place of love and acceptance. You and I need to be intentional to create a space of peace, respect and honor. Leading does not mean dictating. Leading means we go first in loving and accepting. We initiate peace. We show others respect and we show honor. You get respect when you show respect. Your family at home will slowly begin to mirror what you are, not what you want.

Whatever role you have in your family dynamic, you can make a difference. While you can't control what happens, you can show up ready to invest. You can bring health and life. When you show up at home, you will begin to see small changes in the tone of your family. You can make a difference in your home. It takes you to lead.

EXTENDED FAMILY

Your extended family may not live in the same house as you, but they are part of your life, mostly at holidays and birthdays. This is another venue where you can take initiative to lead. Family members gather for Thanksgiving and choose to sit over on the coach watching the football game alone, uninterested in the other family. Some family members who are immature may hold long-time grudges with other family members, which keep extended family from ever gathering together at all.

This is where you come in. This is where you show up. While you can't force it, you can show up with healing, forgiveness and care. Instead of just sitting alone watching the football game, you can get out of your seat and re-connect with other family. This isn't about you. You are not doing this because you need this personally. You are doing this because you have a sense of responsibility that you are entrusted so you can invest into others. You are finding ways, even if small, to serve, love, and heal. You don't just attend family gatherings. You *make* family gatherings.

WORK

Show up at work. Alright, you know you have to show up to work, at least if you want that paycheck. But, are you really bringing your best self to your job? Do you like your job? Yes or no? Do you hate your job? Somewhere in between?

> It's not what you get from your job. It is what you bring to it.

It really doesn't matter if you like your job or hate it. It's not what you get from it. It is what you bring to it. You could be washing cars out in the sun and actually find joy in it. You could be doing data entry sitting at a desk for 8 hours a day and find significance in that. Sure, the work itself is taxing. But you have a lot to be grateful for, much to thank God for. God has done a great work in your life. He is still working, still creating. You have been entrusted with a special calling on your life, and you have a lot to offer.

Jim Rohm, the late Motivational Teacher said:

Don't confuse your profession with your purpose

Your job may have some tedious work, but your life's work is thrilling. Your workplace may have some difficult people that you have to work with or work around. But your heart is to love them and help them. Meet them where they are. You may not have the title or position you desire, but you can be that position now. Don't wait to be given responsibility. Take responsibility. Show up every day with a good attitude, a rested body and soul, and a courage to do what others are not willing to do.

Work willingly at whatever you do, as though you were working for the Lord rather than for people.
Colossians 3:23 NLT

CHURCH

If you believe in God, you ought to believe in Jesus Christ, His Son. (John 14:1.) If you believe in Jesus, you ought to follow Him. Part of following Jesus is being an active part of a local church. A church is not a building. It is not like a club or a membership. A church is a group of people who follow Jesus so they can become more like Him. *You need to be in church.* You need to BE the church. Don't just go to church. Don't just attend church. LEAD in your church. Make church healthy and productive, so that other people can belong to your group of believers.

I am challenging you to teach your family that together you will make church a central part of your life and rhythm. You will not attend church every once in a while, when it is convenient. The church is the body of Christ. (1 Corinthians 12:27) In other words, we implement the heart and mission of God. As Jesus walked the earth loving, healing, and teaching, He revolutionized a culture that was broken. Jesus brought light into a dark world. Now we, as His followers carry on that work by being the church. We look for ways every day to share God's love and light to people around us. We change culture by sharing God's Word and modeling the life of God's Son, Jesus Christ.

You can tell I am passionate about this. I am a Pastor professionally. But I am a Christ follower purposefully. I believe in the church. I grew up in the church. I am healthy because of people in the church. Now, I feel a responsibility to be the church so that others can know God's love and God's plan for their lives.

Show up at church. But, don't just show up. Show that *you are* the church.

NEIGHBORHOOD

It seems that there are never enough leaders. There are never enough people willing to help, willing to serve. When there is a problem to solve, few people have the know-how to bring the solution. No, I find too many people approaching me for advice needing my help. Sometimes, people in my neighborhood simply want to talk. Blow off some steam about work. I have had so many neighbors stop to talk with me and my wife as we were walking our dogs. The conversation starts casually. Soon, they start sharing of struggles they have and the disappointments they are dealing with.

Not everybody in my neighborhood is a leader. Not every neighbor contributes positively to our neighborhood. I have realized that our neighborhood needs someone to show up to connect and to care. This is not a role I desire to take. As a Pastor, I have enough people I look after. However, I see the great need in my neighborhood. So, I have committed to being available and helpful.

One evening, my wife and I were walking our dogs around our community circle. A sweet couple would always stop us to say hi and pet our dogs. Both were very sweet and outgoing. On one occasion, the conversation turned from casual to concerning. The man shared his bout with cancer. His wife filled in the details of the stages and circumstances they were dealing with. As she shared, the man began to cry. It was as if he had been holding this pain in, trying to stay positive. He could no longer keep it in.

I hugged him and then asked if I could pray for them. Neighbors were standing around out in the front porches that night and watched as the four of us huddled in the middle of the street praying. The neighbors knew Jim and Trudy and were aware of his condition. However, they did not quite know what to say or what to do.

This couple that we prayed with were so thankful for our care. Other neighbors thanked me days later for how we cared for them. Two weeks later, Jim was taken to the hospital as the cancer had worsened. The neighbors found me to let me know. I could see a group of them were so concerned. So, I offered to go to the hospital and visit Jim and Trudy. Before I left, I invited the neighbors to pray with me for Jim. We gathered on someone's front porch and joined hands to pray. As I finished the prayer, some had tears in their eyes. Likely, they had never experienced the presence and love of God in a prayer circle like that before.

Now, all of those neighbors who I prayed with on the front porch are actively caring for Jim and Trudy. It's almost like I started a little church group among those neighbors! Previously, they knew each other casually. Jim later went on to be with Jesus. We had a beautiful celebration service, with all of the neighbors joining me to love on Trudy and the family. That day, a neighborhood became a community.

Notice that at no time did I insert myself or push God to my neighbors. I simply made myself available by being present in my neighborhood. Walking our dogs and being kind and approachable was all I did. And, when the opportunity arose, I connected and cared.

> Better to do something and say something, than to do or say nothing at all

A Pastor whom I served under years ago taught our staff this important lesson that I want to share with you. He taught that when someone is going through a tragedy or a disappointment, many times we don't know what to do or what to say. So, we do nothing. We say nothing.

Pastor Rich Guerra coached us "better to do something and say something, than to do or say nothing at all. Otherwise, the person who is struggling feels like no one cares."

Don't forget the "mission-field" of the neighborhood you live in. Could it be that God sovereignly placed you there? If so, then look for opportunities to connect and care for people. When you sense a person is in need, show up. You may not know what exactly you can do. You may not be good at saying the right thing or praying the right prayer. But, for the cause of Jesus Christ, say something. Your neighbor needs someone. That someone starts with you.

COUNTRY

God Bless America. Yes sir. I am patriotic, for sure. God Bless America is not just a song, it is a prayer. Our Country was founded upon the principles of God's Word, the Bible. Our Country was founded upon the belief and the recognition of Almighty God.

When you have found victory in your life, particularly in an area that you have struggled with, you have a sense of gratitude. You know what it was like to be dealing with a struggle. You know where God brought you from, and you remember the work you put in to get where you are today. Live with that same appreciation and awareness of the great Country of America that you get to enjoy. Not every country is as blessed as America. Not every Country affords you the freedoms and protections we get to live in.

I am challenging you to do more than just take pride in America. I want you to do more than just pray God Bless America, or sing it on the Fourth of July. I want you to show up. I want you to speak up. Make America great. Keep America great. Protect your Country. Serve in your Country. Am I actually advocating for you to get in to politics? Yes. I know that is a hot topic that can get us in to trouble if we are not careful. I am certainly not for speaking negatively about other people or other parties. I believe we should keep rhetoric honoring and respectable.

If you don't show up and speak up for the Godly heritage and Biblical principles that our Country was founded upon, who will?

> "The only thing necessary for the triumph of evil is for good men to do nothing."
> —Edmund Burke

Our freedom is not free. The blessings of God are not automatic. We must lead in our Country. We must be active in public discourse. Too often, we have been guilty of letting others with un-Godly and un-Biblical philosophy speak out. Others have been strategic in teaching our young people in education venues their doctrines that question God and question the Bible. While they have a right to speak freely, so do you!

Your role will look different according to your God-given gifts and personality. Some people will fit better serving behind the scenes. Your voice may be heard by how you help with voter registration. Others will support candidates as they run for office. But, every one of us must contribute to keeping America free. Let's not just pray God Bless America. Let's ensure that God will continue to bless America. Our future generations depend on it!

Conclusion

Wow. There is a whole lot more, isn't there? You thought this book was just going to help you overcome your struggle. Feel like this chapter just helped you turn a page? I hope so. I want to eventually get you off focusing on your struggle and yourself. I want to eventually get you to focus on your purpose. I want to show you that there is so much more God wants to do through you. What good is healing and wholeness if you do not have a greater purpose for it?

I know as you finish this chapter, you likely are far from where you want to be in dealing with the struggle you are facing. You are still just beginning some of the shifts in thinking and changes in habits that I have talked about. Don't be too hard on yourself. Welcome to life. This is hard work. Keep working. Keep getting up. And don't wait until you are "fixed" to begin showing up. You will never fully arrive. You will never be perfect. A.A. famously teaches **progress, not perfection.**

You can actually start working on showing up while you are still working on yourself. In fact, as you start showing up at home, family, work neighborhood and Country, I believe it will aid in your strengthening! Understand this: you are not just strengthening for your struggle, you are strengthening for your purpose. God is making a new person in you!

This means that anyone who belongs to Christ has become a new person. The old life is gone; a new life has begun!
2 Corinthians 5:17 NLT

Chapter 10

Yes

The power of yes.

Saying yes is scary. It is exhilarating. Yes, invites the unknown.

The word yes has a profound effect.

Do you want freedom? *Yes.*

Do you want to lose weight? *Yes.*

Do you want to become stronger in an area of weakness? *Yes.*

Do you want to learn to overcome a physical challenge? *Yes.*

OK. So, are you willing to do what is necessary to get there? ...... *pause.*

Are you willing to take one step at a time? ..... *ummm*

Are you willing to start immediately? ..... *let me think about it.*

If you have ever experienced failure, you know what follows yes. The road that begins beyond the door of yes is difficult. The climb is high. Lots of room to struggle. As a result, you have become slow to utter that one easy, yet important word, yes.

You must understand that your journey will never start without a beginning. And your journey will not continue on without continuing to say yes over and over again. When everything inside you is saying no, you must say yes.

A Spirit of Yes

A key to your success is yes. In fact, THE key ingredient I would say is having a *spirit of yes*. All of the coaching I have shared in this book is rendered powerless without it. For you see, without the desire to say yes, you will never be driven enough to start embracing the steps necessary to start your journey. You have to want it. It has to come from within you, without anyone talking you into it.

Leadership Coach, Dave Anderson teaches leaders how to hire the right people for their organization. He believes that while most skills can be learned, there are a few qualities that cannot be. He labels these as the *non-negotiables*. One of these non-negotiable qualities is drive. Dave Anderson says that a person must have an internal hunger and desire that drives them to want to succeed.

Dave Anderson shares of a conference where he was teaching a team all of the non-negotiable qualities one must possess in order to become successful. After the teaching session was over, a young man from the group approached Dave during the break. "Mr. Anderson, how do I get drive? I just don't have a lot of it." Dave looked back at him with a funny look. He responded "honestly son, I don't know. I can't help you. Please step away from me now. I don't want to get the sickness you have."

Ha! When Dave Anderson shares this encounter, the audience always responds with laughter. This story is said in jest. I'm pretty sure Dave is exaggerating here for effect. Following the funny encounter, Dave makes this point: if someone does not have the drive inside of them to want to be successful, nothing and no one can put that in them. While coaches can inspire and encourage, they can't teach growth and freedom to someone if that person doesn't hunger for it bad enough.

I have endeavored to make this book both a motivational book to inspire you, and a practical book to teach you. In this final chapter, I want to invite you in to a journey of discovery. I want to make this very personal. Maybe thus far, you have been reading as an observer, keeping your distance. You thought you may just dip your toe in the water to check the temperature. Now, I am presenting you with a question. I am singling you out among the audience. My question demands an answer. You are being brought on the stage, exposed with nowhere to hide. All eyes are on you.

Do you want freedom in an area of your life? Yes or no?

You think, well of course. Yes.

The next question...do you believe you can get freedom in this weak area?

I Can

What helps us answer yes is having more than just desire. We must have belief. What keeps us from stepping up to the stage shouting yes is that our mind is shouting back at us. We talk ourselves out of answering yes. Is it laziness? Could be. Is it past failure? Most assuredly. Maybe we have had others tell us "you'll never be able to do *such and such*." So, we have this old tape playing in our heads telling us that while we would sure like to see it happen, it is just not realistic. We are simply dreaming.

I have had many great mentors and leaders in my life. One Pastor who led me in my twenties helped me acquire a can-do attitude. Pastor Albert Padilla was a mature, developed leader whom I was brought under. I loved Albert because he encouraged me and inspired me to dream big. However, Albert would often correct me, something I didn't necessarily want, but needed.

I worked hard building ministry in the church. I loved it. However, I often found myself getting stuck in conflict and frustration. When I would meet with Pastor Albert and share my complaints, he would interrupt me with a quick response "Matt can-do." He would then build me up saying how God had anointed and gifted me. Albert would pray for me and love me well. I would leave his office feeling encouraged, but not feeling like he addressed all of my concerns. Later, when Albert would catch me criticizing or complaining to others, he would walk up behind me, place his hand on my shoulder and say in my ear "Matt can-do." This time, it was not an encouraging comment. It was more of a corrective reminder. Albert was really saying "Matt, stop your complaining. Get a better attitude. Move on from the negative and get moving toward the solution."

When I would see Pastor Albert come around, it gave me a sense of accountability. He was loving and relational, but he was also teaching me what self-leadership was. Matt can-do. That was code for "stop telling yourself you cannot and start believing you can do."

> Stop telling yourself you cannot and start believing you can do.

If Matt can-do, so can you. I'm not asking you to jump off a building. No one is asking you to do something stupid. Rather, I am asking you to do something that you know is healthy. It is good. I am inviting you into a greater life, with bigger possibilities. I am calling you out of pain and into God's promise. But it takes you having a can-do attitude. You have to interrupt yourself every time you begin rehearsing an old tape of past failure, past hurts and past people who told you that you would never overcome your struggle.

You can grow stronger. *You can* be healed. *You can* suffer through the process of growth. Whether God chooses to remove the struggle or allow it to remain, you can choose how you view it and what you do with it! *You can!* Yes, you can.

I Will

Yes, I will. God has given you the unique gift of will. What sets mankind apart from all of His creation is our ability to choose. Beautiful. Scary.

If *I can* demonstrates drive with belief, *I will* demonstrates decision with commitment.

Motivational Speaker, Mel Robbins has built a thriving career based on one powerful principle she learned while experimenting with her own struggle of fear and apathy. She shares how one morning she was sleeping in and thinking through the lack-luster life she had. She was frustrated with disappointments and failure. She was stressed with all of the bills piling up and pressure coming at her from all sides. Mel explained how she had wanted to start turning her life around for a while. She knew that successful people get up early in the morning and start their day right with vigorous exercise. Healthy body, healthy mind, healthy emotions. But every morning she tended to talk herself out of getting up early.

Mel said that one morning, she imagined a rocket ship getting ready for lift off. She heard the countdown clock sounding off. She told herself when she counted down to 1, she would jump out of bed. 5, 4, 3, 2, 1, liftoff. She jumped out of bed, put on some workout clothes and started off outside for a morning walk. Mel used this clever little mind game throughout the day. Whenever there was something that she had to do or should do, she would count off 5, 4, 3, 2, 1, and then propel herself to do it.

Mel Robbins calls this concept her 5 second rule. Her research has shown that people tend to talk themselves out of doing difficult tasks. The reason behind this is that our minds are programmed to protect us from danger. When our minds see something that is going to inflict pain, our mind tells us to stay away. This is a survival mechanism that cautions us from real danger. However, our mind can also work against us when we are confronted with a choice to do something that we know we ought to do, but know it will involve pain and suffering.

Mel's 5 second rule says that whenever we are confronted with a choice, we likely have about 5 seconds before our mind talks us out of doing it. After approximately 5 seconds, we will resist making the right choice and default to comfort and safety. Counting from 5 to 1 and then launching out catapults us into making the right choice before we have time to question it.

Having an *I will* decision will catapult you into making the right choices that will ensure you overcoming your struggle. *I will* needs to follow with *I commit*. Commitment is difficult, not something that comes naturally. In fact, you will may have to use Mel Robbin's 5, 4, 3, 2, 1 and then physically force your body to move. Don't feel too bad if you do not have a strong will. Our will is limited. It is like a smart phone battery. It may start at 100% fully charged in the morning. But by the evening, it has drained. That's why your night eating is out of control. No charge left in the battery to resist. In those times when you are simply drained, use this 5 second rule to jolt you to follow through on the healthy habits you are committed to. Thank you, Mel Robbins! What a great technique.

Not My Will

Let's go back to Jesus and the scene at the Garden of Gethsemane:

> Jesus went out as usual to the Mount of Olives, and his disciples followed him. On reaching the place, he said to them, "Pray that you will not fall into temptation." He withdrew about a stone's throw beyond them, knelt down and prayed, "Father, if you are willing, take this cup from me; yet not my will, but yours be done." An angel from heaven appeared to him and strengthened him. And being in anguish, he prayed more earnestly, and his sweat was like drops of blood falling to the ground.
> Luke 22:39-44 NIV

Jesus had a strong *I will* mindset. But we see how He attached His will to the will of His Heavenly Father. Jesus submitted His will to God's. Why?

Jesus understood that following God's will invites God's

> Following God's will invites God's power.

power. God has unlimited power. God sees the end from the beginning. He knows His plans for you. Not to harm you, but to give you a hope and a future. (Jeremiah 29:11) Where God guides, God provides. I know that is a cliché preached in the church, but it is so true. It will be true for you as well.

I think we forget that God is with us. He is for us. And when we make these bold statements of *I can* and *I will*, we are inviting the power of God into our journey. Every time you step up with an *I can* attitude and an *I will* commitment, God's favor steps before you. He clears the way and makes your path straight. When you cower from taking your next step, God is still with you. His grace is there to catch you. But, God's favor is *always forward*. God's voice never speaks from your past. His voice calls from your future. Listen for His voice out in front of you, not behind you. God loves you where you are, but He loves you too much to leave you there.

Yes **Moves You**

Yes is a beginning. Whether you are saying yes for the first time or you are saying another yes, *yes* moves you.

Yes forces an action. It breaks inertia. Something clicks in our brain when we say yes. Questions become powerful tools. They force an answer. Whether we answer out loud or not, it gets us thinking. Questions activate our mind. It jolts neurons to begin to swirl and thoughts to begin to process. The power of *yes* is that it is an act of stepping over a line. We literally are moving from one position to another position. Maybe we did not physically move. Maybe we have not taken action, per se. But our thought process did. *Yes* begins the mental process of *I can* and eventually *I will*.

Yes starts a mental process:

Admittance ➤ Acceptance ➤ Belief ➤ Decision ➤ Commitment

Yes forces movement inside of us:

Mental ➤ Emotional ➤ Spiritual ➤ Physical

Movement creates life. Idleness results in death.

Yes is dynamic. *No* is static.

No is not a bad word. In fact, *no* is powerful and is very helpful. I talked a lot in this book about resistance, guardrails and parents. *No* is a good word that produces good things. We do not say yes flippantly or freely.

But when we recognize God is calling us to fulfill a dream of freedom and destiny, we can lean in to saying yes with confidence. When we say yes to the freedom and victory we desire over our struggle, we begin to move forward in a positive away. *Yes* is the start. And *yes* will continue us on.

Visualize

I want you to *see* how freedom and health are possible. In fact, visualizing your freedom over your struggle is exactly what you need.

One technique that successful people do to reach a goal is they spend time visualizing it. Athletes are taught to first see themselves performing to perfection in their sport. Coaches instruct their players to practice first seeing it, then doing it. Basketball players first visualize the ball falling perfectly through the basket before they shoot the ball physically. *Swish.* A professional diver visualizes the body motion and shape they will move in before they step off the diving board and twist in the air.

Visualizing is a powerful technique we can use in our lives. We can first see it, then believe it, then start doing it. For if we do not visualize success and freedom, it makes it very difficult to achieve it. Experiencing success would only happen in an arbitrary, happenstance way, if at all. Visualization creates a picture to focus on. It creates shape and clarity of what we wish to achieve. When we first take time to create an image of freedom and victory, our mind, body and soul can grab hold and eventually capture it.

What do you visualize? Do you simply allow images to crowd your head? What old tape are you playing of failure and pain? Maybe you would respond by saying you don't think you have any vision at all. I would argue that is not possible. You see, we are visually driven by design. God gave us eyes to see. What we see with our physical eyes eventually becomes what we desire and believe. All of us have images playing through our minds. That is why it is so important that we are careful with what we allow our eyes to see.

The eye is the light of the body. If your eye is good, your whole body will be full of light. If your eye is bad, your whole body will be dark. If the light in you is dark, how dark it will be!
Matthew 6:22-23 NLT

This verse reveals a powerful truth. It says that if our eyes are good, we will be full of light. What does it mean for our eyes to be good? When we see good things, we become filled with good things. When we look at what is good and true, we will be filled with what is good and true. But if we are constantly allowing bad things to be put in front of our sight, we eventually are led downward toward lies and darkness.

We are designed by God to have a vision for our life. God gave us eyes to see. Our body cannot be useful if our eyes cannot show us what we are doing or where we are going.

Vision is not just seeing what is in front of us physically. Vision is seeing a future and a destiny before us spiritually. Look at this scripture reference in the Bible:

Where there is no vision, the people perish
Proverbs 28:19 KJV

Where there is no revelation, people cast off restraint;
Proverbs 28:19 NIV

With no vision, the people perish. They die. The NIV Bible version gives more colorful meaning to the same text. It says that a vision is really a revelation, a *revealing*. Without a revelation, people cast off restraint. This is insightful for us. If we do not have a vision for our life, why then inflict rules and guardrails? Why go through pain and suffering? It's just not worth the headache. Might as well just do what we want. Stay comfortable. Do what feels good now.

Vision For Your Life

A re-occurring theme that is woven throughout this book is the power of having a life vision. While this book teaches how to overcome a struggle, the greater revelation is in discovering a vision for your life. I hope you have been catching the coaching I have been giving you. That is, to not focus on your struggle. Rather, focus on your success. See your freedom. Visualize it. When you visualize this great new possibility of freedom, you achieve great new insight. That word, **insight** suggests having vision *inside of you*. God has put gifting inside of you. He has a seed of potential that He has planted within you. He has breathed His Holy Spirit on you. He has given you all of this for a reason. God has a holy purpose He wants to work in you and through you.

When we begin to see the greater picture God is framing in our lives, it sheds more light on how God is working through our struggle. If we just focus on the struggle, we are left with the pain and desperation. But if we pull back and see what God is designing, we understand a beautiful story unfolding. A story of faith, obedience, and vision.

Plus God

Left on your own, your vision will stay limited. When you count what you can do, it is small. When you include God, your vision now becomes unlimited, expanded. Many of us are used to being independent. We do work on our own. Maybe we like to be in control. Or, maybe we have been disappointed with the lack of support from people.

God does not disappoint. He will not leave us stranded. No, rather, God speaks. God shows up. And when we understand that, we can expand our vision to include God. We can take the limits off what our life can be and what we can do, because God is with us.

You see, your problem is that you have been planning without God. You have trying to dream through a narrow telescope. You need to begin to add God to the equation. That's right. Take what you have and what you are, and then add God to the spreadsheet of your life.

Maybe it has been hard for you to say yes with confidence and commitment. It's not that you lack the drive like the young man admitted earlier, but you just don't believe you deserve to desire a life of freedom and vision. When you accept the realization that God is ready and willing to walk with you through your journey, you can make that declaration. Your lips can actually begin to form that scary and unspoken word that starts it all. Yes. Yes, I can. Yes, I will. Yes, I see a greater vision for my life.

Conclusion

I am so proud of you for getting through this book. This book has really been a journey. A journey of self-discovery. What are you made of? Where do you come from? What has God put inside of you? And what are you doing with it?

In order to answer these questions, we must wrestle with the struggles in our lives. For it is the struggle that keeps us stuck, holds us down. Left unattended, they grow silently in us, like cancer beneath the surface. They grow heavy, like baggage we are having to lug around through life. And while dealing with our struggles is painful, not dealing with them is tragic. It means that we can never fully realize the potential and vision God has waiting for us. We normalize around our struggle rather than overcoming and becoming.

Friend, I wish I could say a prayer and your struggle would simply go away. Disappear. Whoosh! Gone. No, not going to happen. Why does God choose to sometimes let your struggle remain? Why does God not remove the thorn in your flesh? Weakness. Abuse. Sin. Limits.

In my life, I have had my struggles. Thank God, I have found liberty in some areas. That's why I can confidently write this book as a testimony to you. However, I still have other struggles I am working through. Please don't think I have this all figured out. Are you kidding me? No way. God has allowed some struggles to remain in me. God is still working on me. And it is so beautiful to see God's hand on my life. The Potter's hands are forming and refining the clay. Just to have the Master's hand touch my life is a blessing, even if He is shaping and correcting.

As I close out this book, <u>Struggle</u>, I want you to know I am praying for you. My heart is for you. I get great joy out of helping people process what God might be doing in their life. That is the Pastor in me. I have so enjoyed writing this book. I count it an honor that you would share in my experiences and listen to my insights.

Allow God to use your struggle to grow you, build you, and work through you. Dare to dream. Desire and design. Get a vision and then add God to it. He is with you. He is for you.

So am I.